Voices from The Sitka, Alaska Wordsmith

Book 2 of the Martin R. Strand, Sr. Trilogy

iUniverse, Inc.
Bloomington

Voices from The Sitka, Alaska Wordsmith
Book 2 of the Martin R. Strand, Sr. Trilogy

iUniverse books may be ordered through booksellers or by contacting:

iUniverse
1663 Liberty Drive
Bloomington, IN 47403
www.iuniverse.com
1-800-Authors (1-800-288-4677)

ISBN: 978-1-4502-6918-6 (pbk)
ISBN: 978-1-4502-6919-3 (ebk)

Printed in the United States of America

iUniverse rev. date: 11/18/2010

DEDICATION

This book is written by Martin R. Strand,

a Kaagwaantaan man named K'wách'

In memory of our ancestors and Tlingit elders

Kiks.ádi & Kaagwaantaan

and is lovingly dedicated to our grandchildren: Lila

Denali

Gary

Ben

Tyler

Shelby

FORWARD

Pat Sheahan

My friend Monty Wilson went to school with Martin and would almost always comment after an encounter with him, that, "he has always marched to the beat of a different drum." Martin Strand came off at first impression as peculiar. Known as Brother Martin he had a way of presenting himself at first with comedic one liners that disarmed and made new acquaintances feel comfortable. But it also made an impression that he had a silly disposition. In fact, Martin was observing and reflecting and appreciated everything and everyone around him with an astute sense, guided by the conviction that all were important, even sacred.

First impressions are often deceiving. Martin belonged to many groups and to many people. He didn't always enjoy being front and center, however. Rather, he participated in his complicated social world with the ironic eye of an outsider looking in, simultaneously showing solidarity and yet sometimes feeling himself partly outside and on the margins. It is that rare combination, albeit contradictory, that gave him that blessed gift of poetry and artistry.

As to his work, Brother Martin is significant because his words and the images he captured represent an important but confusing time for some Sitkans, especially those that are residents year round over the course of decades. I will try to explain. Martin was "old school". He belonged to the Alaska Native Brotherhood (ANB) because his grandfather's heart "bled ANB".

This group is itself an interesting combination of people, holding to tradition and embracing modern realities. Martin was a man in two worlds.

On the one hand, he was never as animated as when we went hunting and fishing in the traditional grounds around Sitka Sound. There he hunted seal and recalled trips with his family to fish camp when he was young. He took pride in his status at Dog Point Fish camp, where he had a bedroom dedicated to him for when he would come to teach any student who was interested in catching and preparing salmon. Martin taught me about marksmanship and ethics and friendship. We reloaded ammunition together and told stories and dreamed about future excursions.

What we caught, we shared. And we went to ANB meetings together. It was there that I witnessed his allegiance to his clan and to the memory of those Native peoples that had gone on before him. Martin's identity is tied to the Kaagwaantaan clan and nothing made him more proud than that affiliation.

But Martin was a Renaissance man, too. He grew up in the cottages of Sheldon Jackson College, somewhat separate from the traditional native neighborhoods of Sitka. He may have been only a mile away, but Martin would pay a price of this separation by being on the fringes socially. The reward, however, was the chance to be mobile and to expand his opportunities.

He motorcycled across Canada and the U.S. He went to the University in Ohio. He learned piano, hustled people in pool halls, took up photography. At home, Martin ventured into radio broadcasting and computers. He enjoyed bicycles and socialized in any place that might be susceptible to a story in exchange for a cup of coffee or tea. He took up the art of peacemaking and mediation.

And he watched things carefully, documenting people, times and events with an eye toward tribute, not judgment. He was as apt to quote a French philosopher as he was a Native Elder. Watching Martin watch others, I have often wondered how those seas of influence converged in his mind. I believe he used his crafts as a way of maintaining sanity and letting things stand on their own merit. And we are the recipients of his creative compartmentalizing. Creative endeavor is by nature both limiting and expressive.

Martin Strand will also be remembered for being friendly. When I had coffee with him, I was amazed at how many people he knew by first name. He related to the young person serving ice cream at McDonalds' with the same level of attention he would as someone with notoriety in town. He was gentle and saw the best in people and situations. The topics he wrote about and the subjects he photographed related to the average person in town.

And that is what made Martin so exceptional. His industry and unpretentious personality gave voice and honor to what others deemed ordinary and unworthy of celebration. We need caring people to help us see the intrinsic beauty and value of every day life. We needed Martin to be with us and yet apart so that he could respond to the cadence and syncopation of rhythms that at first seemed contradictory and tense.

We needed him to help us to stop, consider and find meaning in the routines of life. Martin marched to the beat of a different drum, but it was the cacophony of sounds that his town, state and nation provided him. Now we can reciprocate as friends do, by listening and learning from him.

AN EXPRESSION OF APPRECIATION

If Martin were writing this expression it would be as long as one of the books of the trilogy. It would include grandparents down to grandchildren, and every family person in between. It would include those whose eulogies have been presented in the third volume of the trilogy. It would include teachers, professors and students related to his formal education along with those who aided him in his cultural learning. It would include the Eagle and the Raven elders whom he held in great respect. It would include those who participated with him musically, or over a cup of coffee, or in camp activities and particularly those who aided him in his medical battles. Every fishing buddy, along with every hunting buddy along with every 'gatherer' would be included. It would include every citizen, or clan member of Sitka, a unique city located in Southeastern Alaska, the beauty of which can not be equaled. Martin was never exclusive.

As the editor I would like to thank Marcia for her long hours of search for his writings, his pictures and her holding together of the family. Our thanks is extended to James Poulson for the picture of Martin, to Henrietta VanMaanen, to Ronald Williams, to Dawn McAllister, proof-reader and occasional editor, and to Dick and Judy Marcum for their technical computer skills. And I extend to God thanks for the ability to put Martin's thoughts together in these books.

Sincerely, Ken Smith, editor.

Contents

CHAPTER 3   SHELDON JACKSON INFLUENCE 101

CHAPTER 5   MUSIC MAKES THE MAN. 185

THE INTRODUCTION

BUILDING OF THE BOOK

Like a fish out of water I struggle to breath the breath of purpose.
The possibility of my poetic work to reach a larger audience
Has a strangeness of feeling that it might eventually happen.
It never was my intention to put out a book of my work.
That there are so many hoops I have to jump through is confusing to
me.

I can see the value in such a project for my family and friends.
I wonder what universal appeal my work could express to others?
What in my poetic attitude would others see of value?
Most of my effort is written on the same day of the event.
The writing comes easily knowing great people I know.

Being a 'memorial poet' is perhaps what I do best.
I rarely write about my own condition but feelings about others.
I am not one to think on my feet as I have to taste my words.
I get messages from my Tribal elders for reading my poems.
They seem to think I should be more spontaneous expressing myself.

In the beginning of the day I want to be original in my speaking
The people I meet in my travels deserve something new.
I try to formulate something different in every day greetings.
"How are you?" they ask.
"Fair to poor with gusts to disgusting" is my quick reply.

1

A dramatic life appeals to me in meeting friends and others.
Why not add something extra special in our daily walk?
My mentors have played an important part in my life.
I will speak in colorful ways without current vulgarity,
Lots of reading sparks my communication skills.

In my formative years I excelled in speech and music.
Missionary contacts lead the way to long for excellence.
Perhaps, involvement in my church taught me to speak well.
Radio and TV work caused me to learn great habits.
It was a continuous learning journey I learned to love.

A long list of mentors paved the way to my eventual work.
Every success I had gathered much praise from my Elders.
My church, in not so subtle ways, guided me forward.
Mother Lila, highly educated, gave me the inspiration I needed.
She exposed me to the world's finest piano music.
I often think of my life as a whole city.
My precincts of thought wander down streets and alleys
Filling my mind of poetic thoughts on a daily basis.
I can scarcely leave my front door without capturing a picture.
My camera, an extension of my mind reaches outward.

There is a question about the camera images I make.
It is in an historical nature I photograph the passing scenes.
The daily changes that move from season to season thrill me.
This year, sadly, I missed the important shore bird migration.
So tuned to Nature this is part of my life style.

The poetic side of images gather in my dreams so often
In picture and word they visit my life constantly.
I often wonder if I am wordsmith or camera man.
If I am to publish my work which one will be dominant?
Can I combine the two efforts into one publication?

These are some of my thoughts flashing past my mind today.
Your help, dear reader, is much appreciated by Marcia and myself.
I have many questions about making initial efforts in this regard.
The machinery of it all attacks my mind in urgent ways.
But it is a bright ray of hope in presenting my work.

Martin R. Strand

CHAPTER 1 ALASKA NATIVE BROTHERHOOD, SISTERHOOD

*Prior to the formation of the Alaska Native Brotherhood (ANB) in 1912
in Sitka, there were many fellowships of men and also women in the local
Presbyterian Churches of Southeastern Alaska. These fellowships elected
officers, conducted meetings and had an agenda that included Bible
Study, social issues, fund raising and often many of the duties assumed
by churches. There were also many social issues discussed and acted upon.
Each of the local fellowships was encouraged by the missionary in charge
of that station.*

*Therefore the twelve men, along with Marie Orson the secretary, who
organized the ANB were experienced in the procedures for establishing
membership, the election of officers and the establishing of an agenda.
Mainly the agenda at first was citizenship and also schooling, but also
included fishing rights and the use of Native language.*

*At the time of the formation of the Alaska Native Brotherhood the local
community groups were called camps and the number assigned to each
Camp was its line of order of joining the brotherhood, as also is the case
in the formation of the Alaska Native Sisterhood in 1923.*

*The organization joining all the Camps is the Grand Camp which meets
once a year in November and normally the executive committee contains
the past Grand Camp Presidents, along with Grand officers of the ANS,
which provide for continuity. As the missionaries moved the organization
was thrown upon its own resources and it has maintained a strong
place in the society of the Indian population. Martin was very actively
involved in the life of the ANB, and was often a spokesman to it and
occasionally from it.*
Ed.

THE ARRANGED MARRIAGE
WE CALL GRAND CAMP

It was the building.
It was the church.
It was the room.
It was the people.
It was the Grand Camp mission that drove me here.

This arranged marriage we call Grand Camp
Put together by our grandparents so we could see.
Oh, the love that binds us so close to one another.
How we wish our offspring could be here.
Spirits bounding off the walls all around us.

Uncle Walter (*Soboleff*) calls out the remembrance of Founders.
At the name of each a candle is extinguished.
Lovingly extinguished by people of Now.
Lives brought here serving a mission.
Lives reliving the beauty grandparents must have known.
A Kaagwaantaan musical warrior makes his way forward.
Halting steps, a mind choked with emotion.
He dedicates his work to worthwhile people in his life.
Not knowing what is about to happen, he starts out
"Piano help me speak to the ones I love" he says.

In the most serious moment of my life I strike the keys.
The sum total of my life breathes a theme.
I remember bygone messages from grandparents.

WORKING FOR ANB

For Ralph
Time well spent, a life well lived, he helps his people.
He centers his thoughts on work that needs to be done.
Giving is his chief component to move the Tribe ahead.
This Kaagwaantaan's dreams are full of vision.
He feels hurt when things do not get done.

There are so very few who understand the ANB as he does.
I lament my light committee life in that regard.
Our friendship is like a cable of steel with thousands of strands.
I hope he feels the devotion I have to his cause.
Our central goal for ANB is strong and more committed.

Somewhere down the line we must meet with a Peace Maker.
The bad feelings have to stop and I hope we get help.
I have hope we can all work together once again.
Personalities in conflict weaken ANB for going forward.
We must unite in this time of crisis before it's too late.

I have watched with interest the many good things done.
Your contributions to ANB have always been significant.
I admire the depth. Your writing speaks volumes of care.
You have been on point many times at meetings.
I regret that I have not spoken up in your behalf.

I wish we could have open meetings to all members.
We have trouble having a quorum often and this would help.
I would fight those that are using the rules as a weapon.
The lack of resources has put us all at risk.
If we get bingo going I want background checks for workers.

What can we do to make ANB active again?
We must have an interesting program every week.
We have to have reasons for people to join.
Our spirits need to be lifted to a new high place.
We are spiritual beings with human experience.

I regret I could not answer sooner.
Last Tuesday I was taken severely shivering from band.
Flu fever hit me hard but I am recovering.
Be assured our friendship is for the long haul.
There is nothing to change that in my view.

THE GRANDSON OF A FOUNDER

Founders Day and the mission of the Alaska Native Brotherhood are one and the same. All my life I've known the focus of the Founders and I learned it from my grandfathers, John Newell and Ralph Young. I am the result, for better or worse, of their cause. I like to think I'm a better person because of what they worked on to make a more perfect, fair lifestyle.

There were role models everywhere for we children. Peter Simpson, powerful man of faith and a boat builder. Walter Soboleff, close family friend and promoter of The Way. Elsie Young, caring grandmother and advocate for a better life. My mother, Lila Newell Strand who knew what we had to do to survive in a changing world. And what an exciting changing world they all worked toward. Alaska Native Brotherhood and Sisterhood were established and moving forward in their mission to gain recognition of Native rights for us as citizens, winning the right to vote, integrated public schools, working toward helping aged Natives get relief and housing and working toward getting equal rights laws and initiating Tlingit and Haida land suite.

Sheldon Jackson School also provided the atmosphere and operations arena through the good will of the Presbyterian Church. The Cottages were an extension of the goals and dreams of those recently converted to the Christian ideal. Our house on Kelly Street was used as a center for the Founders to discuss the issues of the day. I can remember many times hearing meetings downstairs with Peter Simpson, Mark Jacobs Sr., Frank Price Sr., Andrew Hope, Ralph Young and others talking about convention action in the past and up-coming resolutions.

As for the backbone of the ANB, I would hear the women singing hymns into the night with my mother on the piano. Mother would bring up goodies left over and prepared by grandma Elsie for the Ladies Aid Society.

My mother, Lila, was given the piano with our first gold money from the mine by my grandfather, John Newell. My mother soon learned to play it and performed often at the ANB Hall. Her daughter, Sofia Strand Porter, performed at the tender age of 8 at one of grandma Elsie's Social Hours downstairs. I have always been surrounded by good music and I played sousaphone in High School and ROTC Band at Ohio State. Of course the keyboard and piano have always had a special part of my life.

As a boy I spent valuable time at a Kaagwaantaan subsistence camp north of town at Nawkawsina Bay. It was in the Fall of my 8th or 9th year I boarded the "Smiles" with grandpa Ralph Young and grandma Elsie and headed out to fish camp. I can remember no more exciting time in my young life. The roar of fish jumping day and night was such a noise I could hardly sleep anticipating the next day's fishing. Grandpa Ralph made me a light gaff pole with a trolling spoon hook on it. There were always disoriented humpies along the shore for a young guy to gaff.

At night we would eat partially smoked coho heads and tails with rice. My job during the day was to scare away bears for the lady berry pickers and I carried a Crisco can with little stones which I would shake vigorously. The bears would leave the berry patch. I learned from my Founder grandfather the value of providing for others and our future by preparing the food of the land.

Grandma Elsie prepared the meals that would be a close part of my life from then on. Fish head stew with salmon eggs and potatoes, seal and deer heart and liver dinners. Berry fruit cocktail. Clam chowder and crab dinner. The "Smiles" was the longest boat in the Universe. The smiles, a 'mile' between the beginning and the end.

I suppose we children were insulated from much of the local prejudice of the time by being involved in church and school, but we knew it was there. We were always praised for our accomplishments by family and friends and so we benefitted from the goals of the Founders just in my own lifetime. For quite a few of us in the Cottages we had a thirst for excellence and that provided the drive to stay in school and be challenged to look forward in our lives. The Founders were a musical group and many were in the Cottage Band with Al Gordon as the director.

They knew the value music brought to uplift the spirit to a higher plane. This goes way back in our Tribal music history and was a natural common denominator to Western Cultural music. We saw the beauty in the music Sheldon Jackson school presented.

The Founders were a courageous group taking risks with themselves and their loved ones in the time of cultural clash. They were survivors that brought us many of the benefits that we enjoy today. I hope we, the present inheritors, can look to the vision of the Founders to guide us to the future with strength and wisdom. Thank you!

WHAT ANB MEANS TO ME

At this moment in my life!
A lifestyle of continued beauty and challenge is foremost in my thinking. This is why I continue to write and be inspired by my work. The past two years with the Alaska Native Brotherhood and Sisterhood have brought me a rich understanding of those lives around me.

It has been such an honor being 2nd Vice President and my spirit is lifted to a sense of duty and gladness to serve where I can. Our group has covered many compelling topics and great service to the community while on my watch. It's been great being led by President Gerry and First Vice President George Paul. It amazes me the depth of their grasp of our issues. President Gerry is involved so totally in our community and is a credit to ANB. The founding Fathers and Mothers would beam with pride at the quality of his work.

We are, essentially social oriented people. Like the early Tlingits of old we enjoy being artistically together in our songs and dance. Ancient rituals are carried out with confidence and respect. There is tragic beauty in our grieving for those lost. There is celebration also in the contributions of their lives.

We are food gatherers and that is why Subsistence is so important to our lives. I've taken part in harvests from the land since I was eight years old, North of town. My Elders made sure I knew the reasons for taking fish, game, and plants in their seasons. We Kaagwaantaan warriors were well suited for the great outdoors. Of course, we also loved peace. Sharing our harvest with others in the community was always a priority.

It has been my honor to serve with the Dog Point Fish camp in the Spring and Summer. Under the watchful and caring eyes of John and Roby Littlefield I've gladly spent many seasons teaching the young some of my hunting and fishing skills. The camp teaches responsibility in a Nature setting that is second to none. It is not far from town but surrounded by fish and game. Our Tlingit cultural values are important components of Dog Point. Many Elders share their vision and experience with us as role models to the young. Their stories around eventide near the campfire are what makes our work special. It is a community backed effort with help coming from several organizations and businesses.

VETS

They came forward proud for having served their country.
We praised their efforts as they marched by.

Each of us touched by their stories of war to peace.
I remembered my brother Buddy leaving us for the Army.
He left high school early in order to serve.

The entire stage front was filled with veterans at attention.
Collective lives surviving conflict and remembering those lost.
From fronts all over the world they hold in their minds.
Some at times shared their grief and joy and others did not.
So personal is part of their lives we dare not ask.

Today is dedicated to paying tribute to all who serve.
The veterans want the Veterans Display moved to the ANB hall.
It was taken away from Sealaska building.
A motion to their effect was adapted amidst applause.
The families of the veterans stood up behind them.
We salute those from ancient times to the present.

Their direct efforts supported our march to freedom.

NEVER A LAST DAY

October 9, 2004

We turned a new page, a new life to bring forward.
After our fear and dreams collided in a trying year.
The Tribe gathered here today is strong and full of hope.
Survival with compassion has drawn us together.
Our children are beginning to understand our way.

My tears of joy at the young dancers performance was uplifting.
Thankful hearts united in the moment of praise.
Our beautiful lifestyle is threatened occasionally.
We have the tools to fight for justice and eventually peace.
Our Elders speak to us from beyond their lives.

The smoke slowly rises from the smoke house.
Delectable aroma fills the air with tastes familiar to us all.
The late run coho are running and I gaff one in the stream.
We bring them to grandma Elsie who is joyous at the sight.
Grandpa Ralph takes the eggs to prepare caviar.

Grand Camp meant so much to Ralph and Elsie.
I am beginning to understand their depth of devotion to our people.
I saw it only yesterday on the convention floor, so sensitive.
This is the life that was meant to be.
This is our land and our life.

My relatives are so vast in numbers and quality.
They have always made me feel like true royalty.
Loving extensions forever reaching our lives in encouragement.
This is what I remember of my many Elders.
Lifting my spirit without complaint to new heights.

Tonight I reach out and share the best of my life.
Not to be forgotten are those here now.
The candle lights their loving faces.

FOUNDER'S DAY 2006

January 29th

Thinking of our Founders has always lifted my spirit.
Over the decades I have had the good grace to meet some of them.
I would imagine they felt welcome at the John Newell house.
As I was a child then young man, they were frequent visitors.
Early on I noticed that they were always held in the highest esteem.
Peter Simpson would sit with grandpa Ralph Young for tea.
Andrew Hope would be there for meetings right on time.
The ANB faithful also were entertained at our house.
Mark Jacobs Sr., Andrew Wanamaker, and Jimmy Williams
Had strong opinions looking at our problems of the day.

My sister, Sofia and I would come downstairs on occasion
To listen to the various events taking place.
They always made us feel welcome and listened to us.
Our mother, Lila, would often play piano for the crowd.
Grandma Elsie busied herself bringing treats to the visitors.

The issues of the day were magnified in their importance.
The founders wanted to give their children a fair chance.
Moving into the modern world was one of their priorities.
Education was the key and they fought for it.
There were stumbling blocks put in their path.

We are the products of their detailed hard work.
We have come a long way but we have a long way to go.
Our struggle continues and we must have strength to go on.
We gather here tonight to commit ourselves to our goals.
Full of positive hope for our Future.

GATHERING AT THE HERRING ROCK IN SPRING

March 4, 2002

Advancing into each season we pull ourselves ahead.
This is part of our Tlingit nature taught by our Elders long ago.
Our Founders day is carefully planned around the Herring Spring.
It means we gather like the herring around our Herring Rock,
The Spiritual Rock of the Great Spirit who gave us to lean upon.

Sitka supplies our Nation with fresh herring eggs this time of the year.
Our strength comes with our sharing our ocean's wealth.
We were bounteously blessed with plenty of our lifestyle resources.
It was not an easy battle to keep Nature's supplies coming here.
Strong people fought long and hard to keep what we need.

Our Founders were a complex and dedicated group of people.
The will to be free began long before 1912 when ANB was formed.
Our Elders knew what was happening and devised a plan of action.
Today we are the result of that action carried into reality.
Our ANB Hall brought the debate into sharp focus for our cause.

The Founders had much input from the communities at all stages.
They were not alone on the journey in seeking justice for our people.
Grateful for the small, victories grew into larger victories.
The power we enjoy today was carried by the footprints of our past.
Sacrifice of our grandparents early on was no easy path.

Today I am close to the dream of Ralph and Elsie Young.
I look at their lives as inspiration in my own life's journey.
They are out there leaving a light on for me.
This is why this day is so very special each year.
Beautiful lives that made a significant difference for us all.

TLINGIT & HAIDA'S 70TH

My report on the Ketchikan Convention to Sitka ANB. April 21, 2005
Also my 70th year

Lifting my spirits to new heights I reach higher.
Meeting those of yesteryear is the plan.
Aged faces crack with joyous smiles, including mine.
The familiar becomes itself the reality of life.
Happiness looms high on the horizon.

This gathering, this meeting of minds surrounds us.
I feel the greatness of the spirits that have been released.
My grandmother's clan leans forward in wisdom.
My grandfather's people give me the Tribal warmth.
The building vibrates with energy my blood has known.

Is it any wonder that I should confront the past so soon?
My 70th year beams as a broad smile so wide.
My life seems to be on the brink of something good.
I relate to others with such depth of sincerity.
It is like I have lived my life only for this moment.

An ancient Haida prayer lingers long and deep in my mind.
Our prayer maiden spoke it with such conviction yesterday.
The ages seemed to melt away at the simplicity of the poem.
"We live our lives with our own strength."
It was the most important moment to me at this Assembly.

Into the serious business of today began and stayed with us.
How we care for each other is in high priority.
Our reason for being here is understood more clearly.
Insistent voices speak confidently to persuade us.
How we relate to each other is part of our journey.

Stretching the depth of my thinking comes often.
I am challenged to new avenues of thought by Elders,
They speak with a smoothness of their life experience.
We take their words to hear and go on.
Traveling on the same page is exciting.

TIMES OF STRUGGLE - MARTIN LUTHER KING DAY

January 17, 2005

We are no strangers to times of struggle.
The vision of our Founders paved the way for our success.
We were too young to understand the fight that was building.
Our Elders' keen minds and strengthened resolve led the way.
Decades ago the light of freedom was dim yet growing.

I see the moonlight tonight.
I look for the sunshine.
I feel sadly the darkness.

A night time burst of light full of hate and horrible sound.
At Memphis 1968 speeds a bullet across the way.
I read the news fresh off the teletype to the radio crowd.
Realizing we have lost a National hero for freedom
And a wave of terror washes across our land.

I see the moonlight tonight.
I look for the sunshine.
I feel sadly the darkness.

Martin Luther King is gone and Sitka grieves as the others.
We remember the right he fought to lead us to the light.
Our Native Elders saw the commonality of his struggle.
Alaska Native Brotherhood and Sisterhood wept on that day.
We too had gone through the dark side of prejudice.

I see the moonlight tonight.
I look for the sunshine.
I feel sadly this darkness.

My Sitka grandparents fought for a better life for us.
Ralph and Elsie Young walked hand in hand to ANB and ANS.
Each Monday night building a life for the grandchildren.
Our founders were wise enough to capture that vision.

NATIVE AWARENESS PARADE

November 24, 2003

The growing pride in every step today along the street
With such a host of well wishers pleases the ANB.
Community unity has a strength pulling together as we do.
Such willingness to join our parade warms our hearts.
The beat of the drums is a reflection of our joy.

Walking together on life's journey has always been our goal.
Each Monday night my grandparents, Ralph and Elsie Young
Walked with determination from the Cottages to ANB Hall.
I have followed this walk also in their memory.
It is a walk full of meditation to serve the better good.

It is heartening to see the young also joining us today.
Our future will bring them forward to take our place.
We cherish the beauty of their lives each and every one.
Grandparents' ancient eyes sparkle anew at their being here.
The strong joy I feel reaches beyond my years in hope.

Our veterans walked tall today as they always should.
We remember their lives of sacrifice for freedom's cause.
We walk to support our troops living in harm's way.
Our flags wave with pride in their memory at this moment.
The band plays a rousing march in their honor.

The walls of this Hall echo our happiness of our friends.
The powerful beauty of your lives is so welcomed.
We hope to meet with you often down the road of life.
May the Great Spirit bring sunrise to your hearts.

MY WORLD

Wednesday night, September 26, 2001

Reeling my life line, my catch is revealed.
Sorrow overcomes me as I see the new death.
How could I have done such a thing as this?
Stiffened by death my fish is one of my dreams.
A sad lengthy passage from Rachmaninov whispers to me.

Breath is slow and measured as I regain my composure.
Reason overcomes the moment recently sad.
Gathering up what dreams I have left is my goal.
Everything was not lost, just close collateral damage.
My heart still beats in its loneliness tonight.

Chemicals taken for my own good pull me forward.
The doctor offers encouragement and is full of hope.
My treadmill exercise is successful and better than the last.
1966, my year of decision, is long gone and I recovered.
So close to death at that time I remember it well.

My now life has much more purpose than before.
I spend my time much more meaningfully with quality.
My friends are so close and make a difference to me.
I see with much more humility and tolerance today.
Reaching out to others is easier and as it should be.

Two golden eagles visited my life today near the Park.
Proudly on the rock one sits while the other soars by.
Thousands of seagulls are taking their pre-nighttime flight.
A kayak--bucking wind mixes with the rain as salty mist
Sprays my lips 100 yards from the sea's edge.

Grand Camp is close and I hear my name called to go.
It will not be easy to get to be a delegate this time.
Oh! The precious moments for the last two times.
Can I distinguish myself enough to my peers to be chosen?
If I can't go I still have my work with my band.

ALASKA NATIVE BROTHERHOOD AND TLINGIT HAIDA ARE MIXED

Tlingit & Haida Report May 14, 1997 ANB Hall

This eagle, this Kaagwaantaan, this Silver guy, nourished myself in Tribal joy in Anchorage at the Tlingit Haida Assembly April 16-19. A refreshing drink of proud, cultural ways greeting us every day and all day. Central Council listens to us from the floor and through our resolutions about our concerns for our People. "Sovereignty - Yesterday, Today and Forever" was the overriding theme of the 62nd Assembly.

From Angoon where my Grandmother, Elsie Dwee Newell Young was born Angoon delegate, Matthew Kookesh Jr. asked me during breakfast one morning, "Why do you come to Tlingit and Haida Assemblies?" I told him it is my way of keeping my culture alive by being involved and renewing Tribal ties with those people that have been close to our family consistently over the years. As a boy I remember the great Founders of ANB having dinner at the John Newell and Ralph Young house in the Cottages.

You'll be hearing details about the National Welfare Reform program that is coming up fast and how it affects Indians everywhere. I attended this workshop and the powerful presentation of Norm De Weaver, Teddy Wright, and Sharon Olsen. They seemed to think that the rural areas of the State will be hardest hit by the Reform System. A video produced by Central Council will be available to each local board.

Mark Jacobs, Jr. gave a stirring report on Indian Country and Ms. Heather Kendall-Miller from the Native American Rights Fund kept us up to date on the Indian Country (Venetie) Issues and how we will continue to fight in spite of the State's anti--Sovereignty stand bolstered by the one million dollar war chest.

Poem by Martin Strand

I have spent my life clawing at the edges of Glory.
Recalling bygone days of Tribal Splendor and Vanished Glory of
fighting times.
My Kaagwaantaan side has a new mission to be competitive in kind
and caring ways.
We came from Sitka with open minds intent on change.
Our delegation from various walks of life was a working machine
Bright eyed and smiling to all.
We wanted to help others as a team for the communities.
Our Tribal extensions once again gloriously renewed.

APRIL 19, 1999

April 13th through 18th, Juneau was the perfect host to Tlingit &
Haidas.
Meeting old friends is always a joy and inspires the highest human
ideal. I'm Kaagwaantaan (Kogwanton) from Eagle Nest House
(grandma Elsie's house). I am also the child of grandfather, John
Newell (Hoonah) from Snail House. I would mention these facts to
my tribal relatives and they would nod approvingly.

1999 was a sad year for the Kaagwaantaan. We lost the most of any
clan at our memorial service on Saturday. We would give money to
our favorite Tribal fund. I honored my mother, Lila, my dad John
Strand and brother John Bashore (my mother's first child) We would
read the names of those lost in 1998 and extinguish a candle. We
have lost many more this past year.

Tuesday night was the gathering of the Tribe at Goldbelt Hotel. They
had hors d' oeuvres a king would be proud to receive. My favorite was
scallops wrapped in bacon strips. There was a cheese cake with a tasty
spearmint leaf on top. Tribal extended family greetings went on into
that night. All in walking distance from the Driftwood Lodge.

Wednesday night was the Grand Banquet at the ANB (Alaska Native
Brotherhood) Hall. The young Tlingit & Haida dancers entertained
us with not a dry eye in the house. We're proud of the renewed
cultural fire that is going through Southeast Alaska. Jackie Johnson
gave a sensitive and caring keynote speech around our theme:
"Keeping our children safe through Cultural values."

Thursday morning was the beginning of our serious business. Cultural joy and problems were discussed in great detail. Thoughts of resolutions and visions for the future were eloquently expressed.

President Ed Thomas was impressive in his handling the work of the Assembly. I hear many times from delegates he was an excellent choice to lead us. He defused many a side tracking issue in a respectful manner. Cathy and Ed also put on a Hospitality room at the Prospector that was extremely well done.

JUNEAU AT TLINGIT & HAIDA ASSEMBLY, 2000

Impressions cutting deep into my past as a Kaagwaantaan.
I show much of my true self before the assembly.
They encourage my thinking with my clearly defined writing.
I feel the Ancients' presence with such power.
As we deliberate into uncharted, unspoken waters of feelings.

The sense of glory of fighting times comes to mind
As we debate the important issues facing us today.
We have our differences in how to better the Tribe.
The more we complain equals the more we care.
We move onward like warriors have done before us.

Amazing how the issues remain the same and unchanged over time.
Hideous racism in its ugliness is more subtle today.
Manipulated in similar ways we try to find answers.
Governmental roadblocks meet our warriors today.
We see the problems more clearly now, but how to avoid them?

Our host and hostess bring dimension to our gathering.
To hear where they have been is sometimes unsettling.
The problems they have overcome smarts our minds with reality.
Evelyn Edenso at age 90 guides our thoughts in revealing ways.
George Stevens tells a parable with strong moral.

We elected incredibly qualified people that tell our story.
We are blessed with such a pool of Indian talent.
It's not easy to choose those and deny the others.
We deliver our strength where it does the most good.
And we hope we have done the best for our Tribe.

We have dealt with sadness and with grieving loss.

A desolate picture of the past year of leaders and important people.
They have given their lives for our betterment.
Our assembly dedicated to the memory of the Hope brothers.
And so many others that have touched our lives brilliantly.

THE BIRD TAKES FLIGHT

August 11, 2000

The freedom was unleashed today and the bird flew away.
Years of un-fulfilment vanished today and new eyes blinked life.
The beauty was not just the day outside but within our soul.
The Clinic drew its breath for hundreds of people.
Its destiny assured its reach to the Future and is a reality.

We came from Sitka as witnesses of this event of a lifetime.
Gerry Hope and I come with the blessing of ANB Camp #1.
We've traced this rising star with considerable interest.
The hope of our people pulls strongly toward good health.
A lot of our loved ones enjoy their lifestyle here in Ketchikan.

Our extended Tribal family is enhanced from this moment.
We share life's risks and rewards as Eagles and Ravens.
Collective medicine men from the Past gather in our minds.
Their good medicine binds and nourishes our spirit.
They define the best of being an Indian.

Walking with sparkling eyes through the floors of care given people.
We remember those who have gone on too late to share this day.
Their urging insistence brought this dream home.
We have tears of joy and sadness all at once.
What more perfect combination of emotion is ours to see.

I see the decades of people marching invisible before us.
The visionaries, the foot soldiers, Tribal word warriors on parade.
I imagine in wonder the grandparents who had a big part.
Loving the grandchildren they sacrificed nearly everything.
A cultural moment widens and we begin to understand.

Oh! The dances that "opened the box of wisdom"(1) for us.
Their intensity breathed the life of the Ancients.
We returned once again to our Spirituality for strength.
The beauty of our nature does not let us down.
Pride rides high with this mountain top experience.

(1.) A song composed by Harold Jacobs
inspired by Elder George Davis.

REPORT TO SITKA ABOUT THE TLINGIT & HAIDA ASSEMBLY

This is the dip in deep cultural waters I had always dreamed of.
We take the high ground of the Founders proudly.
We sing and dance as if it
is the last day.
Extended Tribal families unite today with purpose.
With care for the communities of our birth we hear the sorrow of
those lost.

We applaud the new opportunities for growth together.
The Elders' eyes sparkle with something special for us.
A time to catch up on the news from our extended families.
Somehow we are renewed with the power they bring.
What an excellent host Juneau was for us.

The highlight of the first day (Wednesday) was the legislative report
of our Central Council attorney, Phil Baker-Shenk. It was so unusual
to hear what others think about us in the political arena and around
the nation.
It was a reality check on what impression we give to others.
Phil would speak as an insider then later an outsider.
He spoke of the legislative inaction to help us with subsistence issues.
It was far from a bright picture.
Selected for Tribal Host was George Stevens and Tribal Hostess was
Evelyn Edenso.
The crowd cheered at their selection.

Our Wednesday, Welcome dinner was keynoted by Stella Martin. She recalled the forward march of Native women in Alaska. She mentioned all the obstacles our women had to overcome in their lifetimes. Stella Martin is a compelling speaker and we all appreciated her presence.

The delegates were all sworn in on Thursday morning by John Borbridge and we got certificates of election.

President Edward Thomas gave us a multimedia presentation as his report. He reported on all the Council's activities over the past year. This included trips to AFN and NPCAI action.

The tribal trust fund is growing and we've been living off the interest for quite a while. We still have to work hard to keep our heads above the water in the troubled times.

From the Tlingit & Haida Regional Electrical Authority head, Mr. Vern Rauscher reported why rates don't go down even when we get a little ahead. He was questioned and lambasted by the smaller communities for having such high life threatening--rates. One community reported 48 cents per kilowatt hour. It was not unusual for electric bills of $350 to $400 a month.

EAGLE NEST HOUSE

With anticipation our planning for Grand Camp became a reality.
Our connection to our cultural past is alive again.
Tribal extensions are drawn closer as we near Kake.
We gladly bring king salmon, herring eggs, black cod, and halibut cheeks.
The ferry cuts confidently through the water as darkness envelopes us.

Dreaming of the days to come even in our daytime thoughts.
I hope my grandfather, Ralph Young, will visit my dreams tonight.
This is the life that was meant to be at Grand Camp.
Relationships blossom once again in the most positive ways.
The most important Convention of the year is about to begin!

ANB Camp # 1, and ANS Camp # 4 are prepared and ready.
Issues dear to our hearts and minds will be presented.
We will check the consensus of our favorite communities.
We come open and willing to listen and learn other viewpoints.
Grand Camp is the place our grandparents learned to love.

Our heavy thoughts bring us to the Memorial Service.
Some of our elders did not make it this year.
We mention their names in sadness and celebration for having known them.
We have a new and terrific sadness of September 11th.
Americans are united in bringing terrorists to justice.

The Drum and Dance will be more meaningful than usual.
We, the survivors have gathered together another time.
As caring and compassionate people we sing our songs.
Our Drum heartbeat sets the rhythm for the Future.
Accepting smiles and vigorous handshakes throughout the Hall.

For some, Kake is the center of the Tlingit universe.
Most of us have extremely strong ties here to the beautiful people.
My grandpa, Ralph, always spoke royally of Kake.
I come to see my school mate Ray Jackson, from our SJS days.
Many Kake people had their schooling at dear old SJS.
This Eagle. This Eagle Nest house member. This Kaagwaantaan is happy to be here.
I always brighten my mind to take part in Tribal doings.

IN CRAIG FOR TLINGIT & HAIDA 2001

April 19, 2001

An inland sea surrounds us tonight as the tide slips in.
The warmth of the day brought the perfume of Spring,
Cedar that drifts into town on a light Southeast wind.
We are treated with such city-wide generosity.
What a welcome feeling binds us close to Craig.

Today we heard the words of important people in our lives.
Dreams of the Elders sparkled in their minds constantly.
The vision for our People was dusted off and polished.
We were new again in our rich traditions and culture.
Indian pride was expressed so completely.

Collective minds moved together in wisdom.
Our reasons for coming here seemed more clear.
A powerful, young voice lifted our spirits high.
Moving rapidly toward excellence and dignity she advanced.
Seasoned with the real world she gave us hope.

What a story we will tell our grandchildren why we came here.
To fill our cups of pure Indian thought.
To taste what a better life might be for us all.
Living Elders with an intensity in caring and loving ways
Gave us the power we needed to take home.

To hear of ancient ways so beautiful and complete a Lifestyle
brought us to our feet in thunderous applause.
Names of our Founders spoken with reverence
For their contribution to our just cause.
Some of us having heard their words in person.

This annual bonding of our Tribal extended families
Is the reason for much rejoicing in this place.
To see loved ones again from favored communities.
Our assembly of caring, sensitive people glisten.
We hear the drum and gladly we dance.

Our moving memorial service sometimes is heavy with
Grief for those who have ended their journey with us.
We celebrate their lives in deep remembrance.
People taken long before they should have been.
Today's service showed that they shall not be forgotten.

As the Assembly draws near a close we are sad.
We prepare to leave with centuries of wisdom.
Our elders have given an extra measure of themselves.
Rich in Spirit they bless our leaving.

Something special has happened here to remember.

PAUSE FOR CONSIDERATION

There is a new emptiness in our lives today.
My mentor, my help in troubled times has gone.
Mark Jacobs Jr., our 'Tlingit pathfinder,' left us this week.
Today I honor his life force in strong remembrance.
He walks with us in truth and confidence.

I am full of thanks for our ever--evolving School District,
For its cultural sensitivity in having this program.
The civil rights leader, Dr. King, and ANB and ANS Founders
We honor today give us hope for a bright future.

The road to more understanding each other is secure.
Tonight in a cloud filled sky I look for the moonlight.
I have seen the sunshine.
Today in my life I understand the darkness.

AGAIN ON KAKE

Marvin Kadake, past president of ANB, gives us the story of the huge flag that is hung on the Kake ANB Hall. It was part of the town long before he could remember and holds a special place for the people here. Looking at it, it is threadbare and faint red, white and blue-- almost pastel. Native military men and women of the town who have served our country over the decades look to it with pride. Our color guard opened Grand Camp with the posting of the Colors. In his lifetime, Walter Soboleff recalls seeing a flag in Sitka with 13 stars as one of the most rare.

The Drum and Dance will be more meaningful than usual. We the survivors have gathered together for another time. As caring and compassionate people, we sing our songs. Brightening my mind to take part in Tribal doings this Eagle, this Eagle Nest House man, this Kaagwaantaan is delighted to be here. The accepting smiles and vigorous handshakes are throughout the hall.

Bunkhouse Hilton was only a short mile from the Hall. With me there were delegates from Hoonah and Haines. It was great to catch up with their news about Game Creek in Hoonah and Rusty Back Lake in Haines. Ray Dennis, related to Fenton Dennis, was there. A fine young man who came in crutches after knee surgery. Nothing was going to keep him away from Grand Camp. His buddy, Dwayne Wilson was there They wore fine suits and ties. The founders would be pleased indeed.

Each day opening prayers and the Battle Song was sung. A stirring keynote address was given by Niles Cesar, BIA *(Bureau of Indian Affairs)* Regional Director. He related the closeness the BIA and ANB and ANS have had over the years and said it will continue. I thanked the Bureau for its help in starting Strand Photography in 1965 with a grant from the BIA.

The Kake High School class visited us Tuesday morning and I wanted to talk to them about literature and poetry, but there were too many high visibility speakers that morning, namely Gov. Tony Knowles who was warmly received and spoke at length about Katie John's fish weir victory. We gave him a big hand.

We had a lively panel on "Challenges to Local Camps." Many ways to get Camps interested in continuing to grow in membership and projects. Having goals and projects seems to be a good way to go. We need more younger folk.

Summing up my stay in Kake, I am so grateful I had the chance to go there. Our delegation was a contributor to the Convention in many ways. Isabella confronted Ed Thomas, president of T&H about JOM funding and heard the sad news. Nels cultural knowledge shined like beacon on a dark night. Margaret, the politician made some good moves. Fred's points were well taken by the Grand Camp. Pat helped when the alternates were called. Irene gave our Camp the support it needed. Gerry defended our herring issues. Nelson, Camp warrior did well. We were led by Herman in good directions. Me, I was at my poetic best throughout the entire convention.

SYNOPSIS

We started off the Convention Tuesday morning at the Andrew Hope ANB Hall. The most notable moments were when keynote speaker Walter Soboleff spoke about Native Values. T&H president Ed Thomas gave a moving tribute to the late Judy George in still photography with musical back ground and was well received. Wisdom Keepers and Vision Seekers spoke of young and old.

Wednesday the rains came and did not darken our mission at Grand Camp. Coho lunch was on the menu with seaweed soup and rice. I bought three helpings for myself and two others. The Juneau camp cooked coho to perfection. We had our memorial service at the Presbyterian Church. I played my C# minor meditation and it was very well received. Note: my backpack and hat saturated with Snapple were washed by the Motel's help and I picked it up. The Snapple cap was put on wrong and spilled completely in the back pack.

In addition to the Memorial Service there were two remembrances for Richard Stitt and Judy George. There were DVD videos of pictures of their lives, public and private. It was sensitive and well--presented and the crowd was really moved in love. President Gerry Hope presented Camp # 1's donation to the Cyril George Family. Libby Watanabe of Camp #4 presented to Camp # 10 ANS of Kake a Koogéinaa that was gifted to Judy George from Libby's grandfather, Judson Brown. Tlingit & Haida president Ed Thomas reminded us of budget implications of the Katrina Flood and the Iraq war. We will be impacted in reduced income for some of our best programs. It was a sobering report as we are looking down the road.

I dined with four other brothers at the Goldbelt. Our fellowship spans decades of caring for our People. It was not a rare meeting and good humor prevailed. I told the "We the Willing" poem and Ron said, "Standup with me at the installation tomorrow night and tell it."

It was a knee slapper and Dewey agreed. The wide smile of Harvey confirmed. Frank recognized the Tribal Hoonah humor. With all the sadness we've seen over the years we could still joke among ourselves in our fellowship.

It was great working with president Gerry Hope, Clint Watanabe, Isabella Brady, Harriet Beleal and Libby Watanabe for Grand Camp. We will be looking forward to the 2006 convention in Hoonah.

ON TO HOONAH

Now there are many ways to go in
 my life that I find confusing.
  So many things to complete and so
   little time. Reaching out for some kind
    of perfection in presentation or the
    written word. I am hoping to get
     going on several fonts as far as my
      resources can take me. Scraping
       together computer parts to make
        a working model of my best expression.
        I want to expound my knowledge of
         fonts for writing and I have stumbled
          on this one that can say it all for me.

              Tonight the Alaska Native
                Brotherhood and Sisterhood meet for a
                 potluck and meeting, the first of the
                  season. I want to prepare something
                   about my grandparents to present to
                    the crowd tonight. It is not so long
                     until the Grand Camp Convention and
                      I must be visible to the Tribe if I
                       want to be elected a delegate. The
                        Grand Camp is in Hoonah this year
                         and we must start early to work on
                          constitutional changes. The status
                           quo our people want nothing changed but
                            the liberals want it up dated for NOW.
                             It is so great to attend Grand Camp
                              and I want to be there this time!

Martin R. Strand

During the summer I have met with the
staff of the Alaska Native Studies
Program at SJC. They are off to a
running start and it's about time!
Dennis Demmert, Jan, Laurie and
Laura run the project.

A FERRY TRIP TO HOONAH

Into the fading night we rode the moving ferry.
The gentle sea swells were hardly noticed in our glide.
Sitka left behind lights fading rapidly now facing the blackness.
Hearts warm with expectation we gladly looked ahead.
Focusing our thoughts on our mission was our real goal.

The time dripped slowly as the mists struck our window.
The eight second blinked green to the starboard.
The menacing red blinked danger to the other side.
Moving to an ever deep sleep rest overtook us.
Dreams of the good ahead we planned for our people.

The canoe pulled ahead with the strength of ten men.
Dripping water the only sound as the paddles lifted.
Our resting spot for the night only ten miles away.
Moonlight on the shimmering wind swept sea.
Lifting the canoe high up the beach we then rested.

October morning heavy with gray dew droplets everywhere.
The paddles idle under the canoe as breakfast was made.
A faint glimmer of sun lifts over the mountains.
We spoke so softly to each other with deep respect.
Our leader motions his arm to the waiting sea.

We think kindly of the people of Hoonah days ahead.
Our gifts are carefully boxed in the hold for the right time.
Our hunters got three deer and a seal at our last stop.
Their hunting skill is considerable and we are thankful.
Eagles are successful fishing all around us.

A short distance away from Hoonah we pull out and rest.
It is time to prepare for our entrance to the village.

We drum around the final bend and they hear us coming.
Their drum and welcoming songs fill the air.
We have arrived at last at the best part of our journey.

This was written after midnight on the MV Taku heading to
Hoonah. It was so dark all I could see was the blinking red and green
lights of the buoys. I always have dreamed of kayaking to Hoonah
and this is the result of my dream.

SOGGY MORNING IN HOONAH

October 6, 2006

Peeking out into the darkness early one morning I saw joggers going by the Manse where I lived. It is such a joy in this quiet place to think and create. My table faced the sea with a huge tree and falling leaves. It was the morning of October 6th. This poem was not presented to Grand Camp as I planned. Instead, I presented it at the Hoonah Presbyterian Church on Sunday the 8th. I did not have it printed, so I read directly from the computer screen On the piano I played a remembrance of the 1944 Hoonah fire that burned half the town including Snail House.

6:45 A. M. In its quietness soggy joggers pass by the road.
Reaching for some distant goal they run in the dark.
Their dreams slowly becoming reality with each step.
I wonder about my own dream for the day.
Wanting to make a difference in my life looms ahead.

Our disciplined journey takes us in many directions.
Grand Camp, our cherished Grand Camp, has a life.
I revel in the ancient wisdom it brings to the present.
The great lifting spirits our grandparents have known.
I feel this Hoonah presence of my grandfather.

In its special way this sacred land speaks volumes.
I hear the caring, marching warriors of the past.
I see the blessed mothers of our own with their young.
The rain beats a rhythm on a sweet smelling cedar roof.
Lives rise up for the work of the day refreshed.

I drank the cultural waters of joy of last night.
The dance of life in the heartbeat of the skin drum.
The lovingly made regalia flash and sparkle before me.
As if I have only lived for this one magical night.
I will carry the message back to my waiting people.

Strong and refreshed of spirit we plan the day.
Our work takes many challenging twists and turns.
I feel the unity rise up within our lives.
There is a sense of accomplishment building today.
I stand back and look forward at the work of beauty.

WHAT'S IT LIKE AT GRAND CAMP?

The leisure of getting ready to get to the ferry terminal took my own sweet time. Around 10:30 P.M. we headed out the road. I got the okay to board right after I paid $34.00 for the round trip.

The big box of Tacky Tackle was hard to carry. I was assured I did not have to bring it back by Jean. It had been used a few years ago on another Grand Camp. There was a light sprinkling of Grand Camp people on board and some were already sleeping. It was wise for me to bring my own pillow to blunt the wounds of those "torture" chairs.

The hum of the motors deep below me made it easy to fall asleep. Before that I watched the blinking warning lights up the straits, white, red and welcoming green. A Borbridge grand-- daughter and her young child were active. The child crawling quickly away from its mother up and down the aisles. I wondered what it was like to travel by canoe to Hoonah in those ancient days from Sitka.

The greeting committee was at the terminal in Hoonah and took us to the ANB hall. Charles Kingsland was in charge of housing and gave us a berth at the Presbyterian Manse just 50 yards from the hall. What a stroke of luck! It was beautiful and great protection from the weather.

The Icy Straights tourists complex tour was significant. It is the latest endeavor of the city of Hoonah. It recalls the early days beginning in 1912 when the cannery first started. All the main buildings still stood where they had been built. The theme was fishing and canning. It spread over an acre or two West of town. We were served halibut and king salmon lunch with a deluxe salad and cherry sauced brownies. I went to the beach shortly thereafter and demonstrated the art of sling shooting to an adoring crowd.

Charles Kingsland took me on a tour of Hoonah. He showed me all the new developments since my 2000 visit. To top it off, I got to photograph two large bears at the dump.

I talked at length to Willie Jackson, my conventioneer friend over many years. I mentioned his son George married to Dione, is doing good for the community. He was a great help at the Totem raising September 30th, pulling hard to straighten the pole. I had supper with Willie and his veteran buddies tonight and we talked at length about guy things.

Tonight (Wednesday) I present my poem for the Memorial service at 7:30. It combines my 2004-2005 Memorial poems that seem historically fitting for the occasion. It is short and I hope to the point. (Later note: my poem was a success and the ANS executives officer wants me to have it available to all delegates.)

The local gun shop has a model 93 Winchester 22 auto-loader for $275.00. This was my first borrowed rifle from Don Cameron Jr. In the Charlie Bailey house next to the park. I took it up Indian River and shot my first kingfisher, which I regretted later. It is the same model 22 that was used by exhibition shooters like Annie Oakley and Buffalo Bill Cody. They would throw up coins into the air and hit them every time. The sights are low to the barrel for precision shooting.

Thursday, after a restful night at the Manse I took an early morning walk around town. Before anything opened I walked. Then after a while I had breakfast at Mary's restaurant. The blueberry pancakes were delicious.

I sold the Tacky Fisherman Ties to Ray Dennis for $50.00. I helped him label them to give to the delegates. He's working to be first Vice President of Grand Camp. Our delegation is working hard selling tickets for our 50/50 raffle and we got a good start. Camp # 2 Juneau brought forth a resolution # 37 to censure our Grand Camp president for past bad deeds. We spent most of the morning squeezing every bit of negativity out of the issue.

My Sheldon Jackson School classmate, Kenny Grant, took me to lunch today. We talked of the good old days at SJS. It was a refreshing look into long gone memories so deep in our minds. He may have been a freshman and I in junior college at the time. I asked about his brother "Butter" who is on the East coast working with people.

It is Culture night now and I got away just in time to write these impressions. The Mount Fairweather Dancers danced the opening evening event. I have photographs of their coming to Sitka for the 1967 Native Dance Festival. They synchronized three loud drums as their entrance dance. The most colorful regalia was displayed in a dramatic fashion.

Before the evening event I visited the Brother and Sister teen club and put on a demonstration of pool shooting. One young boy got a detailed lesson on what it takes to be a better pool shooter.

There was a heartfelt demonstration of veterans before the dance. A father introduced his three sons with military involvement. One had been in Iraq and was going back soon. Willie Jackson, Vietnam veteran, gave a stirring speech of hope for the young men and other veterans gathered around him in support.

I sat with the Forest Service personnel for the Native Food dinner. Walter Echo-Hawk from the National Native Rights Fund from Colorado was here and I talked to him about casinos run by Natives. He sang a Southern Indian warrior song accompanied by his drum. He showed great artistry in his presentation.

Walter Soboleff, Grand President Emeritus, is here and I invited him to the manse to relax. He sat with a friend that has recovered from alcoholism who related his progress to date. The warmth of the lounge brought out truth in talking for those present.

I had lunch with Charles Kingsland, the Snail House lot owner. We had emergency pizza and soda pop since all the restaurants were full at noon. We sat with a Hoonah family involved in fishing. Their young son busied himself running into trouble in a positive way.

Friday morning I wrote "Soggy Day in Hoonah." It was 6:30 and is all inclusive of my visit to this place. Perhaps at the Sealaska banquet I will read it.

Dewey Skan is our new president of Grand Camp ANB. Johanna Dybdall is the ANS president. I voted for both of them and backed them all the way.

During a break this evening I put on a pool exhibition at the Teen Center. They have three tables but cue sticks are in bad shape. The granddaughter of John Martin was there and is interested in pool.

The prime steak dinner by Sealaska brought Friday activities to a close. In addition the Klawock Kopy Kats (KKK) performed with Elvis (Sensmeir) to a cheering crowd. However, big trouble with the sound system.

Saturday morning I watched a greater blue heron fishing under the window of Mary's café. It took off and it was a large bird. I watched it circle upward to its perch 200 feet in the trees. They sleep at night in the trees away from predators. After breakfast I went to the church and practiced "The Great Fire of 1944." It recalls the Hoonah fire that burned most of the town, including grandfather's "Snail House." I think I will play it for church Sunday. I practiced on the piano again tonight before our Grand March and Grand Ball. It is out of tune but might have some potential.

Tonight I had dinner with Walter Soboleff and his daughter, Janet. We were at the Totem Lodge and the tide was way out. They said they saw a bear the night before not far from the dinner table. You will remember that Charles Kingsland and I saw two large bears at the dump. Janet said she was appalled to see bear living at the dump. The young lady that served us remembers me when she was a girl at Dog Point Fish camp.

We had our Grand March and Adaline de Castro was my escort. Last night she mimed the theme from "Cats" with KKK. The song was "Memories" and beautifully done. The crowd went wild.

My opportunity to do poetry in the Hoonah School system did not materialize. The English teacher was supposed to let me know the times that were available. Another chance gone.

MY HOONAH

My Grandfather, "Koohúk", John Newell was born here around 1860, belonging to Hoonah's "Snail House." He eventually moved to Sitka along with his nephew, Ralph Young. Along the way they discovered the Chichagof gold mine in Klag Bay and enjoyed some wealth for a while, however, never losing their Tribal roots.

John married Elsie "Duwee" from Killisno and their home became Sitka. He helped the ANB founders in every way he could. His boat "Goldenrod" made many trips around Southeast Alaska in ANB formative years. In the 1985 Convention in Sitka, I was given the honor of receiving a resolution naming John Newell as a great supporter of ANB.

When I was 5 years old John died, but I remember as a child coming to his woodshed and seeing his carving room where he gave us kids dry fish snacks. Leaning against the wall was a large American flag, which he proudly displayed on special days of the year. My playmates Frank Price Jr. and Rosco Max Jr. were frequent visitors to his wood shed.

"Looshkát" Ralph Young of Hoonah became my next grandfather when he married "Duwee." They moved into the John Newell house on Kelly Street where I spent my first 17 years. The area was called the "Cottages". The missionaries wanted a place for recently converted families from Sheldon Jackson and my family was part of the initial group.

Like a deep drink of refreshing water I come to Hoonah.
My young family of five came here in 1984 on a quest.
We stayed with Buster and Martha and visited Jessie and George.
I photographed this visit and some day I will display my work.
We put the halibut hook snagger to good use in Game Creek.

Gracie and her boys gladly played with my children.
Sara Joy, Martina, and Martin Jr. ran all over Hoonah.
Our sense of belonging here stays with us still.
I felt this Tribal warmth all during this convention.
This good will has only deepened over the decades.

I enjoyed my stay at the Manse in its quiet beauty.
I did not need TV or radio, just the silent collection of my thoughts.
I felt I was given space to think about my life.
My computer companion busily prompting my next move.
I was allowed to comprehend what Hoonah means to me.

From the Convention I take home valuable lessons.
Lord, give me the discipline of a Sargeant-at-arms.
Let me do what needs to be done in kind and caring ways.
May I sensitively respond to problems of my people.
And let me live my life with more respect that I've seen here.

I made arrangements with Charles to speak at the church service Sunday morning. Saturday night around midnight I composed this piece. It recalls my connections to Hoonah, and it is in appreciation of Hoonah Presbyterians letting me stay in the Manse. I heard a group of Presbyterians from out-of-State built the Manse. It is in the premiere setting in Hoonah facing the sea. Munching on animal crackers later into the night I finished my writing. The church crowd loved the work and my piano music on their ancient piano.

ON THE WAY TO JUNEAU

Our minds in full expectation of being here.
With every stroke of the paddle we come closer.
Caring deeply in our purpose we talk among ourselves.
In good weather, maybe, 15 miles a day we come forward.
Grand Camp is the prize, though distance seems closer.

We travel with the spirit of Andrew Hope, Patrick Paul, Ralph Young,
And Mark Jacobs Sr. Each elder glistens in our memory.
And what a reflection we are of our Ancient Ones.
Our backbone, ANS moves with equal distinction toward Juneau .
We refresh ourselves with fish and game along the way.

The year of planning and deliberation is in its harvest season.
Come here with full respect for our Tribal "extensions."
The salt sea strengthens our lungs and our arms.
The Southeast wind fills our sails and takes us in the right direction.
Soon Salisbury Sound is just around the bend.

NINETY FIRST ANB GRAND CAMP

In Ketchikan October 4, 2003

We brought sunlight to Ketchikan for six days straight. Seagulls flying around in a deep blue but windy sky. At night, a heavy warm weather fog moved in and burned away the following day to reveal the Sun.

Our tribal extensions greeting us with such joy we felt so much at home with them. ANB and ANS camp # 14 were ready for us at the airport all the way to registration hall. We brought herring eggs, salmon and halibut in several boxes.

Herman, Martin and Nels were later joined by Mark at the convention along with ANS delegation: Margaret, Libby, Roberta and observer, Isabella. We were quickly taken to our lodging around town. I was fortunate to stay with the Chester Worthington clan at Tongass Tower. Then later, Jim Davis invited me to the Harbormaster Condo with the million dollar view of the harbor.

We took care of convention business Monday through Friday with half of Saturday off before the installation of new Officers, Grand March and Grand Ball to end our work.

One of the most memorable moments was declaring Walter Soboleff "Citizen of the Century." He, without a doubt, was most worthy of the title and many stood up to speak glowingly about this life. The name of Erma Lawrence of Ketchikan was submitted to UAS for consideration of Honorary Doctorate degree in 2003. She sang with such enthusiasm Onward Christian Soldiers at the beginning of our day. On another day we sang the battle song when the organist wasn't supposed to be there but came in at the last moment. Two horn players were in the back ready to play. The organist had trouble with the volume, it was on the low side. The people up front sang with the organ but the people in the back with the horns were a half tone off. We in the middle tried to correctly sing but the damage was done.

When it came time to select the Convention City of 2004 there were three entries: Haines, Juneau and Sitka. I read the resolution for our invitation and several other camps stood beside us and we won the convention for 2004. Herman spoke of the Kaagwaantaan last potlatch and the Kiks.ádi war with the Russians as part of the program. ANB and ANS will jointly host the convention. Bulletin, Sam Jackson wins another term for the presidency of ANB along with Ray Dennis as first Vice President. Jack Lee from Hoonah was elected 2nd Vice President. Natalie Williams of Kake took the Brotherhood Secretary position. Mr. Paul from Ketchikan is our Sargent-at-Arms.

From the Sitka Camp # 1 Nels Lawson did an outstanding job of presiding over the Cultural Night of Dance. The opening to Cultural Night was impressive with all the Camps represented in the regalia finery as the hall filled up with the drummers and dancers. Ketchikan Intercultural Dancers put on a drumming program to start the evening out in style.

Evening programs included the Klawock Kopy Kats (KKK) in lip-synced musical pieces by three women including Ray Sensimeier as Elvis. The crowd roared their approval. Our first night entertainment saw Hawaiian night with grade school hula dancers in a thrilling display of talent.

I was involved with the Citizenship committee with chairperson Marie Olsen. We considered several resolutions and presented them to the convention. Many of our camp were on many committees and were a credit to our efforts. Nels was on the floor of the convention several times and had points that were very well taken by the crowd.

Archie Cavanaugh of the Vocational Training and Resource Center (VTRC) gave an active presentation about their program. They have impressive Fall courses planned from introduction to commercial

Drivers Licence to computer operation in Juneau. Some of these have special reduced rates for Senior Citizens.

It is Grand Camp my grandparents loved and talked about for months after it was over They also took an historical view of previous camps. I have a growing appreciation, like them, for the floor action and the cultural ritual followed for the many years ago. Walter Soboleff has been our mentor for me and my family for decades. He told me we are related to the Hunter family who were first in Sitka then moved to Angoon through the first marriage of John Newell, my grandfather. My list of Tribal relatives seems to grow larger with each passing Grand Camp.

I want to thank ANB Camp # 1 for giving me this opportunity of a lifetime. Each convention has been a source of cultural growth and inspiration to look into our rich, beautiful past. It's been a pleasure working with my president Herman during this time. I am looking forward to the 2004 Grand Camp and am willing to help get it underway to the best of my ability.

THE 2004 GRAND CAMP REPORT

The months of preparation for Grand Camp came into reality on Sunday October 3rd with delegate registration at our ANB Hall. The exciting mixture of Tribal extensions blossomed with renewed friendships from the many communities. It is truly an honor to be selected to represent ANB. I have not missed a Grand Camp in the past four years and my grandfathers, John Newell (Koohuk) and Ralph Young (Looshkát) lived for Grand Camp as I do now. Through their guidance and effort I had a life easier than before. They paved the way for a lot of our rights and for that I am extremely grateful. Grandma Elsie Young's God--loving life also formed my sister, Sofia's, and my early years growing up in the "Cottages." Being chairman of the devotional committee I was surrounded with choices for our morning devotions and prayer. I presented people's names to my committee and by convention time we had only two changes. Walter Soboleff did the opening devotional Monday morning. The devotions and prayers were right on target and appreciated by Grand Camp. Early on I noticed that the sound system was out of adjustment so I turned down the bass and increased the treble and found revere was set way too high. It worked beautifully after that. In preparation for my committee I thank president Dennis Demmert for his draft copy of devotional procedures.

I tried hard to get a real piano but ended up using my Casio keyboard. We were fortunate to have Kathy Newman of Sheldon Jackson be our accompanist on the piano for our Battle Song. She took time off from work each morning to help us.

An interest in my mind is always the Tuesday night Memorial Service. Our service this year was dedicated to the memory of Grand Camp President Sam Jackson who died in office earlier in the year. It was my honor to do the Prelude in C# minor on the keyboard and also present a memorial poem "A year in the Ocean of Tears."

President Dennis Demmert, George Ridley and myself were delegates along with alternate, Mike Baines. Our faithful observer was Dan Svetlak cheering on the sidelines. Our president and delegates took an active part in the convention being appointed to various committees. Dennis Demmert was particularly helpful with his wisdom about previous conventions.

At the death of president Sam Jackson, the Executive Committee selected Ron Williams to be temporary Grand Camp President. Camp # 1 asked, "Why wasn't the 1st Vice President, Ray Dennis, sworn in accordance with our constitution? The executive Committee answered they wanted the Grand Camp to select a successor to Sam Jackson at the 2004 Grand Camp. A lively discussion took place. As a result the election took place and Dewey Scan was elected Grand Camp President. Brad Fluetsch announced he was moving on as treasurer and the camps thanked him for his years of service with warm applause. Richard Rinehart Jr. was elected Treasurer and Calvin Wilson Jr. of Kake was elected 1st Vice President.

Libby Watanabe of ANS Camp # 4 announced that Clint Watanabe's committee was pleased that the president, Art Cleveland of SJC in appreciation for ANB and ANS long time association of SJC. President Art eliminated all the fees for the Haynes P.E. Center. It was announced that there is interest in starting a new camp in Skagway. It will be called Camp #98 in honor of the Spirit of 98 theme. They are asking for a Grand Camp group to come up there for installation ceremonies. The news brought thunderous applause from the delegates. Juneau put in a bid for the 2005 Convention saying it had everything necessary for a fine convention. There was no opposition and they are the Grand Camp site for next year. Sitka as site for this year's Grand Camp gave the traveling paddle to the Juneau camps and wished them smooth sailing into the future.

ANB/ANS 2005 CONVENTION

There once was a man down on his luck and he asked another man for something. The other man said, "Brother I have nothing to give you." Our man in need answered, "You have already given me something. You have called me brother."
This was the basis of our brotherhood and sisterhood so simply spoken in the opening speech. Walter Soboleff also spoke of the values we should have for our young people to give them a good start in life. We have a complete DVD recording of the keynote address.

Our friends near and far gathered for this incredible convention. My tribal ties were renewed once again, this time with greater depth than before. Home of my grandparents: Hoonah and Angoon were especially important. Angoon came back after being away from Grand Camp much to the delight of the convention. 93 delegates were present.

It was my pleasure to work with president Gerry Hope on our fund raiser. We met with corporations about our financial problems in Sitka. The T&H office upstairs was helpful in letting us use their computers to do the letters.

Under the direction of Harriet Beleal we put together a 50/50 raffle bringing in over $300 for ANB and ANS. The items donated in Sitka brought in money for the Grand Camp and was appreciated by all. Andy Hope III donated his books and Indian Country maps which were sold at Matthew DeWitt's booth. Matthew was also instrumental in our successful 50/50 raffle by selling the most tickets for us.

The most disappointing part of Grand Camp was putting the resolutions off till the last minutes. Many camps expressed their displeasure since the resolutions are the most important reason we come to Grand Camp. Part of the problem was that we are experimenting with having a shorter convention. It used to be six days, now cut down to five. It was promised to consider more time for resolutions in the future conventions.

CHAPTER 2   HUNTING AND NATURE

SEPTEMBER MORNING THOUGHT

Today, in a bright stream of praise I rise.
The sun, at last, burned away rain clouds.
Franz Liszt opens my mind to possibilities.
Forward and confident he presents his story.
Hanging on for the ride I receive a musical blessing.

The computer room still cool before the warming sun.
The cursor impatient for my next move blinks.
I can keep up with its insistence and words flow.
I wrote of the chicken hawk yesterday after crows.
The swift flight darting with great skill I see.

Could it be I missed the shorebirds heading South?
I never missed them before, so what is happening?
So focused on getting ahead time has robbed me.
It is so important I am tuned to Nature
Enveloped to the seasons I constantly seek the beauty.

I speak with words from a time long gone.
Reaching deep into thought they come easily.
I am fulfilling the tasks that destiny has given me.
Each day brings a newness into my lifestyle.
Today I feel something good will be happening.

Coho peeking around the bend catch my attention.
I will be ready when they start their silver jump.
My lures polished and hooks sharpened at the ready.
As in ancient times they lure me to the shore.
The first bite and the fight is on and happiness is near.

And so, this is my story told confidently to you.
I hope you see another side of me and my dreams.
Willing times to write come and go upstream.
My life's window is always open reaching out.
The music in my veins finds a way to the surface.

AT SEA INTO THE NIGHT

The gathering darkness brings the beauty of the night.
Impatiently I go out into the sea with my kayak bobbing.
Splashing waves clear the bow and paddle spray hits my face.
Dipping suddenly the shearwater dives before me.
Dancing moon on the water has a hypnotic effect.

Flipping herring do not seem to know that night is near.
Silver bodies flip and splash and perhaps king salmon circle.
Sea lions roll and they reach the surface where herring scatter.
My course is set for a sandy beach miles away and warm water.
Cool wind winds westward and the waves pick up spray.

Getting away from town is always refreshing to be in Nature.
Winter pages of my life are reaching toward the coming Spring.
The bright music of the sea birds sharpen my reason for going.
The love to be here has a long lasting strength to be alive!
This is my destiny, beautiful and free to roam the salt sea spray.

Clam beach is revealed and they squirt mist three feet high.
Butter clams and cockles are harvested at the turn of a spade.
The low tide is slack for a while when I continue digging.
I see other diggers down the beach with their flashing lights.
Our families will have a delicious dinner tomorrow night.

The Kruzof westerly wind protects my craft heading home.
It is on my back and speeds my progress toward the town lights.
What a night, fruitful for my efforts a paddle past the breakwater.
At the speed I travel I have time to reflect on my life.
What more could any man want for a life so full?

PADDLING OVER MY WORLD

The swift current swept my craft in an upward motion suddenly.
The wind was playing an important part in it's direction.
I heard an otter whistle in the bank close by.
My paddle struck bottom but it was a sandy bottom.
Seagulls hovered almost motionless above me.

I struck a passing salmon while I paddled away from shore.
Two dippers surfaced on my right with their matt gray bodies.
The river slackened its pace nearing the mouth.
Trout scattered quickly in front of me.
Mallards jumped straight up flying into the wind.

The kayak steadied as I approached the seawater.

Black turnstones appeared and disappeared in flight.
Their backs are black and under their wings white.
As they veered against the bright sea they seemed to vanish.
Always welcome are the first birds of autumn.

The Southeast wind was strong and the waves high.
The shallow waters surrounding Totem park neared high tide.
I reached beneath the surface and grabbed goose tongue.
It had a satisfying salty taste and gave me strength.
Two black oyster catchers piped at the shallow point.

Paddling over the clam beds eight feet beneath me I remember
As a child these beaches were safe to dig.
Now we must go far away from the city for the best clams.
The eel grass fields under me were swaying with the waves.
I could see clearly a black bass school feeding.

The trip was close to home, working my way past Sheldon Jackson
College.
It was such a short trip but filled with memories.
It was just an ancient echo of what my ancestors have known.
I was refreshed taking their path today.
The sun came brilliantly out of the clouds as I beached my craft.

GLAD FOR NATURE

Short--sighted with tunnel vision desperately looking for answers.
I breathe slowly as in a trance as the day broadens.
Solutions so distant clouding my mind in mindlessness.
Wanting to make something meaningful of my ancient life.
The birds are outside waiting for me to give them a call.

Stretching forward my cramping limbs hurt on and off.
The cold has something to do with the forward mobility.
The trips into Nature this month are so worthwhile to me.
It forced me to do something I have not done for a long time.
Opening my mind to possibilities in the good, clean air.

The effort was monumental getting into the forest's floor.
Stiffening legs and poor balance point made things more difficult.
Slipping and sliding and falling to the ground was my fate.
Nothing serious but an annoyance none the less.
Both trips I did not have sling or my gun to hold secure.

Off to the cliffs of Beehive Island and deer tracks in the snow.
Monkey berry bush with a great "Y" for the slingshot handle.
Winter wrens whistle a soft warning that we were coming.
Alert kingfisher chatters as our craft makes a cold landing.
So alive am I in such a setting bringing thoughts of early hunts.

Tree harbor reveals no game and I must test my gun in the field.
My single shot shoots a 10"x10" rock near the shore smartly.
The sun is bright and we decide to go to Krestof Island to see.
Through the islands on the way seal were spotted feeding.
Huge granite boulders dropped from the Ice Age are there.

We reach a bay with such incredible beauty with a sand beach.
My World War II binoculars spot a deer feeding at water's edge.
I'm let off and stealthily make my way to the 100 yard range.
To my disappointment the deer had fled to the forest.
I gaze at the offering of Nature and I am glad to be here.

BEELINE FOR LAZARUS

The air was crisp and the sun shining brightly. I took a light meter reading and it read 20 fl. This means I would be two stops overexposed at f8 at 1/1000 of a second. This would be alright for photographing whales and sea creatures. As soon as we left the farthest tip of Japonski (airport) Island we could see many whales. I took some pictures from inside the boat but the imperfect glass windows distorted them. I wished I could have gone topside and done the pictures. There must have been 100 whales in the area. Everyone was fascinated at the sight.

We were making a bee line for Lazarus Island. In the 1960s I was honored to make a trip ashore there with Jack Calvin and Les Yaw. I did some bad images of that trip and it was my fault for not processing the negatives properly. Today was my chance to make up for that mistake. I took a reading with my Gossen Luna Pro light meter and measured 17 fl and I used f8 at 1/1000th of a second from the upper deck. The 28-70 mm zoom would not blur the images at 1/1000th and I used that setting. Also in the distance to the South and West, I could see the king salmon fishing fleet about five miles off shore.

My dad and I fished 30 miles off this coast in the 1950's and often anchored on the North side of the island at night with other fishing boats. There were cormorants, shear waters, and gulls around the island. I remembered the puffins, murres, stormy petrels, guillemonts, black oyster catchers, hundreds of shore birds that abounded on and around this island. Of course this is the winter season and few birds were here today. As we left the island I resolved to return in the Spring and make a landing.

In the 60's my brother, John Bashore, and I would charter an airplane that would drop us off on the beaches of Kruzof and we'd hunt for deer. It was a rare day we would get deer but the thrill of being in a volcanic area was something to remember. I have hunted the beaches with one of Sitka's greatest hunters, Lawrence FB (Fat Boy) Anderson. He knew all the dangerous rocks and swells and we got deer every time. I also hunted with George Anderson here many times. FB used a 22 cal. Center fire rifle. George had a 7mm Russian rifle. I used a 243 Winchester bolt action. My brother's choice was a Model 88 Winchester lever action. Eventually we had bad luck with that rifle because the lever action pin fell out rendering the gun useless, but that's another story.

We tried to time our outings to low clam tides. Kruzof Island has a wealth of clams. Butter clams, Horse clams, Cockels, and Razor clams were in abundance. And low tide draws the deer like a magnet to the seaweed and salt. Mud Bay was also special in the Fall and Winter. We would catch fish in the river and shoot ducks and geese in the bay. A little known place for duck hunting is the large ponds in the interior of Kruzof. The most famous inland duck and goose hunter was Art Petroborg Jr. I talked with him several times about this interesting hunting area.

SUBSISTENCE RESPONSIBILITIES

Circling the globe on a day like this
Negating the dangers at lightening speed
I cringe lowly looking out of thin blinders.
Seeing truths never seen before.
I shudder more violently as I close the window.

Wanting to get so much more out of life
I stall at key moments letting time talk to me.
Looking forward into the wind and rain
Feel against my face I press forward.
The herring swirl endlessly in volume beneath me.

The tide ever rising on the flat plain touches my feet.
The cool radiates up my legs as I wade deeper.
Refreshment comes slowly but it is there!
Barnacle scratches from the rough rocks draw blood.
With shoes in hand I make the other side.

The 223 is chambered, a steady log gives support
The cross hairs at 16 power narrows the target.
The trigger slowly squeezed. I am surprised at the bark.
The full metal jacket is on its way in a millisecond
The seal floats in the blood soaked sea.

Grandmother realizes as I approach the shore
That I have done something for the family.
With knife sharpened well in advance of my coming
She removes the skin and prepares the liver for supper.
The smoke house will be busy tonight.

The neighbors hear the news and come to share.
Each one is given something for their evening meal.
The hunter has taken care of those in need again.
He takes the first taste of liver and onions.
Grandfather nods and smiles with approval.

Tomorrow we go to Redoubt Bay for sockeye.
The 18--foot open skiff is prepared the night before.
The 15--horse Johnson will run for nearly 3 hours to get there.
I busy myself sharpening my Camilus pocket knife.
I will catch 90 sockeye like I did the day before.

We only took the Winchester Model 52--22 caliber with us.
With peep sight set for 50 yards it might bring a seal.
We are not worried about bears - we never worry.
The tide is high as we launch the boat from the beach.
The nearly three hour trip begins with anticipation running high.

SHORE BIRDS

Beginning today I rose with a confidence rarely felt.
The opening of possibilities greater than myself are revealed.
The will to work again invaded my thinking and this is good.
Wanting to do something worthwhile was heavy on my mind.
Could this be the time for my new beginning?

There is so much I would like to do with my remaining time.
Oh, to print again the negatives that have been long dormant.
There is a restlessness about me that grows more powerful.
Doing something that can help others and myself is my wish.
My low energy and stiff body long for more sweeping movement.

If I could catalog my belongings in boxes to know what I have.
"What is so important each day that I avoid working toward?
What is there to stop me from advancing forward in my work?
It is not a question of the time available to do the work.
It is a do nothing mind set that gets in my way, robbing energy.

The shorebirds are late again and I must see them soon.
They are my Spring opening to my world giving me hope.
Their lives are important to me, hoping that they will last.
I have such a longing to be with them, to cheer them on.
It would be a tragedy to let them fly by unnoticed by me.

HUNTING

Slicing through the water in virtual silence the paddle transfers my power into movement. Never leaving water the paddle cuts a small wake. Light rocking right and left is the only motion seen. The deer does not notice my delicate landing on seaweed.

120 yards away the gun bark is not heard and the deer falls. My family will rejoice this evening with a complete meal. Smiling children busy themselves around the table as mother serves. The admired hunter swims in a bright stream of praise. He bought some time into the future and he is glad.

Years as pages blowing in the wind pass since I hunted last. Longing to provide for others is strong on my mind. Refining my shooting at the rifle range takes up my time. I want to be ready to perform flawlessly when the time comes. The waiting for opportunity is the hardest part of my life.

My knives are sharpened for the task at the ready. The stainless steel deer hanging hooks swing empty in the shed. Decades of no use and they begin to have slight corrosion. I polish them in anticipation of just one more hunting day. So many things more important get in the way of my freedom.

To hunt ducks and geese in season blows in the Fall high winds. So many exciting hunts I have known where I have brought game. They're flying South, again the geese honk to let us know. Rusting shotgun on the wall swings when the wind shakes the house. They want me to move to the outdoors to life again.

Many hunting partners gone away to the
Great Spirit grounds.
I remember them well and the great times we enjoyed in rich Nature.
Part of my sadness is not taking them with me once again.

TO BE A GREAT HUNTER

Early one morning my father woke me. "Get up we're going up to the cliffs." he said. He grabbed a box of ammo and took the 30-30 Winchester and we walked across our street and into deep woods. The woods were dark and I wondered about bears. The chill air hit my face as we moved quickly away from the river. Soon we were climbing up the side of the mountain.

Every so often dad would stop and look. He'd sit down low. He said you could see sitting deer easier from the low vantage point. We scared one up and it took to heavy cover. One thing that bothered me was dad would always stop on a slight hill and leave me a step short of looking up the mountain. I thought some day I would be up front so I could spot the deer.

We reached his favorite hunting area, it was the cliffs of Verstovia. You can see them from town about half way up the mountain. We sat in old growth forest and there was a heavy layer of moss all around. He blew the deer call and we waited. Not long after that Dad spotted a deer behind two trees watching us. He said he wanted a head shot as not to waste any meat. He lined up the front sight with the buckhorn back sight on the deer's head. Kaaboomb!

The deer disappeared to the ground. Did we get it? I ran over there and saw that it was dead. After dressing it out Dad prepared it for packing. The front legs were cut and laced through holes cut in the back legs so you could pack the deer on your back. We had our lunch and began the long trip back. That's the story of my first hunt with my dad.

At an early age I always wanted to be a good hunter. I worshiped my brother's skill. He was expert in the military. He was also expert in pistol shooting. He was one of the most careful and skillful hunters I have ever known. Sometimes he would hunt with his friends for deer up the mountain. They would bring several deer down to Grandma's smoke house.

The Model 98 German Mauser was in 8 millimeter caliber. It belonged to George Prescott who was my hunting buddy. We reached Caution Island in Redoubt Bay and made a landing. It was low tide and the morning mist was low. From that vantage point I could see in a circle over 300 yards. There is a stream in two places. I watched over a hundred Black Turnstones fly in formation near the river. Mallards by the dozens washed themselves in the other stream.

I glassed the area and saw no deer. Not to worry, I knew this was a good spot and something would be drawn to the low tide like a magnet. My binoculars soon spotted a beautiful buck making its way down the river. It looked like 500 yards away. As it moved closer I could see it would be out of sight so I decided I'd have to shoot. The mauser sights were in meters so I set them at 400 meters. My first shot hit high. The deer did not know where I was at that distance. Carefully I rested the gun on a mossy rock and let fly bullet number two and down the deer went with a neck shot. The river plane was flat so I paced off the yards and came up with 384 paces. George and I quickly came to the scene and I slit the deer's throat and it bled freely as I began the dressing process. It must have been near 150 pounds. It was a clean kill and I was proud of it.

Not long ago I used to trade guns back and forth among my hunting buddies. I guess 300 guns of various calibers ran through my hands in trades. I never bought a new gun in my life. I've had 22 hornets, 218 Bees, 222 Magnums, 233s, 243s, 2506, 6.5 Sweedish mausers, 7mm mausers, 7mm magnums, all the 30 caliber guns, 338s, l375s, 348 Model 71 Winchesters and others. What would my favorite gun be? Safari Grade Browning 264 Magnum. It would be good out to 400 yards. Once with this gun I shot two geese in a pond with one shot. Kaaboom!

WRITING THE MEANING - BIRDS

From June 16 our trees in the yard have been blessed with a family
of the red-headed-Sapsuckers. Rosy head and breast, speckled black
and white back and wings, and a just right length beak for business.
Near the end of May I saw my first Sapsucker by the walking bridge
of Indian River. I considered myself the better having seen it be it ever
so brief. That same day I told an SJ person about it and they said they
saw one on campus. Was I delighted to have one soon pecking away
at our trees?

I have to tell you that this is not my only bird sighting this season.
One day in May I took Marcia's 10x50 binoculars to Totem Park. As
I walked to the mouth of Indian River I spotted many ducks through
the alder trees which blocked the view. I hurried to a better viewing
spot and sat down to count and observe one of my finest sightings.
There were Golden Eyes, Bluewinged Teal along with Greenwinged
Teal, Gadwalls, American Wigeons, Mallards, American Mergansers,
Pintails, Buffleheads. Rounding out the sighting were several
Dowitches nervously eating along the shore.

My walks to the park began in early April. My first two sightings
were three Greater Yellowlegs. Then abundant flocks of Western
Sandpipers, Ruddy Turnstones, Semipalmated Killdeer, and later that
week Killdeer. One thing I noticed was cooperation of Surf Scooters
and Harlequin ducks. They would form a straight line and dive and
chase fingerlings to shallow waters.

The birds, sadly, are not in the numbers I have seen along Crescent
Harbor and Totem Park when I was a boy. The old Squaw ducks by
the millions would cover the waters. from Salisbury Sound to the tip
of Port Alexander. Their plaintive call would mean Spring is here!
Equally millions of shore birds covered the shores and at low tide all
the rocks in the Sound.

Here's the story of how I became interested in birds. There was a lone apple tree on Baranof School grounds and one day I saw a strange bird sitting on it. Curious, I went to the library and sat for a long time with Birds of America until I knew what kind of bird was in that tree. It was a Mourning Dove! It was over 40 years later that I spotted one near Kelly Street and photographed it with my 600mm lens. It was published in the Sitka Sentinel.

SINGING TALL ON A LOW BRANCH

It seemed such a confusing situation at a tree near the harbor.
Cars full of noise thirty yards away and boat motors loud.
A mother and daughter stopped by the old tree listening.
They moved on refreshed and I wondered why?
As I moved closer I heard a song of such beauty.

Holding its breast up high a robin gloriously sang.
It's song overcame all the calamity of other sounds.
It seemed as if it gave its whole life for this moment.
The cascading trill filled my ancient ears with happiness.
The bird did not stop while I was twenty feet away.

This is what I should do with my life I thought.
I answered with my best robin whistle.
The bird sounded so satisfied with it's life in this place.
I recalled the Shostakovich 5th Symphony's slow movement
The flute solo sounding as if on the edge of humanity.

I moved on in wonder of this rewarding moment.
Not so simple a bird sings such a powerful message.
Sing as if it was to be your last song confidently sung.
The beauty was so much needed in my life nearly tearful.
If I could pass this message to the people dear to me.

It is difficult for me to hear some bird songs.
My hearing far from what it used to be I watch and strain.
Hoping to hear what I need to hear to carry on.
I see the birds high on the tree tops and I know they are singing.
My eyes remember for my ears their busy music.

Martin R. Strand

Chortling raven sounds come from my roof.
The black bird flies to the neighbor's roof and I see it.
Beautiful vocal variety messages it sends out for all to hear.
5 A. M. on sunny days in Totem Park ravens talk
Full of meaning to each other they continue understanding.

MOSS GARDEN

In her mind
Her reflection in the river was less beautiful than before.
I had taken a sudden turn toward, quite simply, old.
All my life I've been a rolling stone.
Now my speed is so much slower and the
Moss looks more friendly.

I can face life with all its subtle meanings more
Confidently, with medical help.
I wondered for a long time why she
Didn't have gray hair
But it didn't matter, really.

Obligations of the day were quickly dispatched
So I would have more time for myself.
Oh! How I longed for more time in the darkroom!
Ancient eyes and tired legs.
Longed for the afternoon nap.

I cried that no shorebirds came here this year.
Am I the only one who cares?
Sometimes I feel very alone
When the shores are quiet, except for the waves.
When will they return?

The amazing youth of our minds pushes us forward.
Making a "come-back" out of little things.
Love seems bigger than ever.
It's the ageless thing in us all.
Small victories lead to bigger things.

Martin R. Strand

We sat next to the sea, wordless
Nothing needed to be said.
Warmth of a hand
And two lives that really sparkled!
There's so much that is worthwhile!

INDIAN RIVER BRIDGE FISHING

Steadily a wave of mist pours over my body as I bike.
The feet are first soaked then the water--proofed raincoat.
My shoulders feel the cold creeping down my arms.
My riding gloves are saturated but fortunately warm.
Riding glasses suddenly are steamed as I approach the forest.

Glistening is the surface of the bridge as my brakes attempt to grab.
Sliding nearly 50 feet I carefully come to a stop.
The bike is wheeled onto the path through Salmon Berry bushes.
I hide it away from public view behind mossed logs.
My blue satchel swings off my shoulders and I catch it in time.

Mists over the water as the river makes an "L" turn.
I stay clear of the river not to scare the fish.
My golden spinner is already attached to my line.
The telescoping rod is expanded out with lure on the tip.
I see silver flashes in the ripples throwing the lure near the far shore.

Letting the stream do the work a Dolly Varden strikes.
A bright pound-and-a-half trout fights for its life.
My eight pound line holds handsomely and I coax it out of the water.
Frisky it darts among the sand and gravel but it's mine.
The frying pan will have it's way tonight.

The trout are about the same size and in excellent condition.
Some tourists on the bridge stop and watch me pull them in.
So easy a place to get trout without a car or boat.
I clean them on the spot with my old Camilus pocket knife.
I load my bike with a bag full and head for home.

This spot has historic memories for me and my family.
My brother, John, first brought me here as a young boy.
Later my dad and I fished the entire length of the stream.
In the Fall I often gaffed and snagged coho at this spot.
And at one time a horned deer sat across the beach from me.

Twenty years ago I saw a dipper (water ouzle) throw it's young down.
Their nest was safe in the struts of the bridge.
Having a camera and out dated black and while film I waited.
The chick climbed up the rocks and I photographed it.
I have an 11x114 print close-up of that wet bird.

Franklin Jacobs and I brought a 10 gauge cannon here to test fire it.
It was in the attic of grandpa Ralph Young's house with ammunition.
The cartridges were high brass loaded with black powder.
We staked it down with cord and fired 25 shots into the river.
There was no bridge here at that time but we had so much fun.

This week I'm taking President Haaland there for trout fishing.
Today I'm doing some scouting to see if the Dolly Varden are back.
If not we go to Indian River dam to try our luck.
My grandson, Benny Mancil, enjoyed this spot where we fished.
Someday I'll take grandson, Gary here to open his world.

THE SALMON BAKE

Tyler, Shelby, Lila, Denali, and Gary full of life prepare quickly.
Eager lives ready for adventure bent on sudden action.
It comes quickly enough as the boat is loaded with over 100!
Pushing the danger limit the little ones hang over the edge.
Watchful parents try to minimize that danger.

Hot chocolate served by the "tip" taking server and we are on our way.
The fun of running up and down the boat stairs is done.
Martin Jr. Records the harbor scene with his camera
Photographing the land and seascape of his young life before.
Some of our relatives have been away since 1990.

Grandparents Chris and Neal bask in the sun of memories.
Martina with watchful eye keeps track of the children.
Dennis engages in conversation with other passengers.
Benny remembers the places Grandpa Martin took him as a child.
A light Sitka wind blows ripples on the water.

Our craft takes off at 24 knots an hour with a small wake.
Captain Cushing of Sitka fame guides the boat with confidence.
Passing Thimbleberry Bay I recall duck hunting before there were houses.
George Prescott and I, guns blazing, got ducks in the small passages.
Tyler and Shelby, eyes sparkling with enthusiasm survey the scene.

Napping Grandma Marcia fades away in a sunny seat.
Approaching Silver Bay eagles are spotted flying and nesting.
Sawmill Cove Complex is met with questions from our relatives.
From the Mill to Industrial was quite a change for we Sitkans.
Sawmill Creek still provides water for the city and steel heads.

All too soon we are pulling into dock at the hatchery with fish
jumping.
King salmon everywhere and frantic charter boat fishermen casting.
They come dangerously close to snagging each other as they cast.
Tangled lines bring about fishing panic when a fish strikes.
Cherie laughs at such merriment as we are tying up.

HUNTING LESSONS

My wet boots are cooling my feet so it is time to turn around.
After hunting there are places we stop to wring out our socks.
And sometimes if we are tired we soak our feet in the river.
My dad taught me this ancient refresher.
Especially when we are packing deer from the mountain.

There used to be rainbow trout in this river.
I would bring my fly rod with Royal Coachman flies.
The Black Gnat was always the trout's favorite.
It is a plain black fly stoutly tied floating gently on the water.
The trout were only 10 inches but tasted so good.

Of all the fishing my Dad, brother, and I did, I miss the jack salmon.
In late September through November they would come.
We caught them at the dam of Indian River.
A spinner or bright lure was all we needed.
About a foot long we would catch over a dozen for supper.

In 1947, a cold winter, ptarmigan (Grouse like bird) were here.
They were driven by the cold weather out of Canada.
There must have been thousands all over Baranof Island.
Buddy and I would easily get a dozen in the morning.
Behind Totem Park was our hunting area and we did very well.

My first experience hunting was with a Winchester autoloader.
This .22 caliber was lent to me by Don Cameron Jr.
We were great outdoor friends and hunted together often.
I shot robins and thrushes along the river and we ate them.
They cooked well with a little salt and pepper.

WALK UP INDIAN RIVER

Shaping my day with a scraper on a raw nerve
I scream in silent pain in the cold of the morning.
The forest, snow falling, brings additional chill.
The wailing of a flying bird awakens my mind.
If only I could openly cry out my fate.

Slices of ice gather in the hem of my trousers.
The East wind stiffens to my crouched back.
Rocks along the river glisten with glaze over with ice.
The merganser darts toward small fish in the stream.
My boot leaks as I cross the water.

The water ouzel's warble finds a little amphitheater.
It is the shell of a large rock that reflects its bright song.
A life always in the cold, how could it sing with so much beauty?
Perhaps, it is telling me to keep my distance.
I take this lesson from Nature with renewed strength.

Three land otters seem to play in the ripples at the dam.
I shot three there in 1956 with my new Remington 22
It was Christmas day and a gift from my father.
They sold for $30 each and I saved the money.
But today I let them live their purposeful lives.

Winter is so alive after the deaths of the wild plants.
Way upstream in the deep pools blackened coho swim.
Early Tlingit used to get them in January for chowder.
I've seen them in December while going to hunting grounds
Only in the deepest pools they can be seen.

Echoes of ravens around the bend calling out.
They search and find food in unlikely places.
Sometimes their voices reflect great character mimicking others.
Their vocabulary is vast and full of expression.
I often caw to let them know I mean no harm.

CHAPTER 3   SHELDON JACKSON INFLUENCE

The official birth of Sheldon Jackson was April 17, 1878 when the school opened in the old Sitka Russian barracks building. The school has advanced as the educational needs of the youth of Alaska have advanced providing excellent education to youth from villages that were too small to provide those experiences. Perhaps the names of the school show this best for it was established as Sheldon Jackson Institute, then became Sitka Industrial and Training School and then Sheldon Jackson School, followed by Sheldon Jackson High school and then Junior College and finally by Sheldon Jackson College. For almost 130 years it met it's goal to assist Alaskan youth to become Competent Christian Citizens. It was closed in May of 2007 due to financial considerations.

Sheldon Jackson was an integral part of Martin's life. He lived in the cottages adjacent to the campus and he walked past the campus daily. He was likewise welcomed often in many of the buildings. Though he attended Sitka High School he had many friends at Sheldon Jackson and later he attended the Junior College. Likewise his family enjoyed the educational community life brought by Sheldon Jackson and personally Martin had many friends in the staff of the school.

Volunteers in Mission (VIM) were very close friends. These volunteers from the Lower 48 usually came for the summer to assist in maintenance of the school though a few stayed for a year of volunteer service. Martin would appear at their break times and he enjoyed their company and they enjoyed his.

Ed.

THE WINDING STAIRS
OF WHITMORE

It was only two years I actually stayed at Sheldon Jackson.
I could have camped out at home but we thought it best for study.
My parents exhibited a lot of wisdom in this decision.
I would be living with my peers and experiencing everything they
did.
I felt a little independence and that was good for me.

I thought I knew everything about Sheldon Jackson, growing up on
the campus.
Through our church I attended Sunday School in most of the
buildings.
The ancient gym was so familiar to me at basketball games.
The huge lawn was good for kite flying and watching migrating birds.
The shorebirds would always find some kind of food for their liking.

As a child I enjoyed sledding from Stuart's Hill to Sage Building.
On icy days we would sled all the way out to the flume on the beach.
In the flume I would catch trout, humpies and coho in season.
Some were too big and we would drag them home to the Cottages.
The skins were scratched but they cooked up real good.

We would listen to many a sermon by President Wurster, Rev.
Elwood Hunter,
Rev. Bromley would speak of the joys of Rainbow Glacier Camp.
My sister, Sofia and I would memorize long passages from the Bible
In order to win a scholarship to Rainbow Glacier Camp.
It was our grandparents wish for us to get involved in Sheldon
Jackson.

We felt an obligation to seek an intelligent life.

The encouragement of our extended Tribal family moved us in that direction.
Role models like George Betts of Hoonah, Andrew Wanamaker,
Walter Soboleff, Gibson Young, Agnes Peratrovich, Andrew Hope,
And Frank Price visited us for the last time when I was 9 years old.

Sheldon Jackson Junior College shall always be close to our family.
My continued education from there was an Administration collaboration.
Rolland Armstrong saw promise in me along with President Wurster.
Les Yaw played a big part in seeing that I met Fred Palmer of Ohio.
Fred Palmer gave me a scholarship to Ohio State University.

As I grew into manhood Sheldon Jackson brought me many friends,
Professor Delaney sparked my fire to learn in depth.
The Prescotts were an inspiration as friends and mentors.
Hard working Bill Bullock also showed great finesse as a bass singer.
Paul Biggens showed me the inner workings of music that I carry today.

Elinor Matters took us to General Assembly in Philadelphia in 1956.
Capt. Laurie Doig took us on a Choir Tour of Southeastern in 1957.
Hendrick Van Dyke was most inspirational to me at KSEW.
I was honored by Elder Andrew P. Johnson to put his Tlingit message
On the air each Sunday afternoon followed by my "Words & Music."

At the death of my father, John Sverre Strand in 1960, Austin Van Pelt
Gave me a job at KSEW as soon as I returned home.
My radio imagination grew with the help of Mr. And Mrs. Hoff.
Randolf McCluggage taught me the art of getting along with others.
Mr. Boles gave me my dramatic eye for poetry.

I met my mate, Marcia, at the Home Economics building & kitchen.
Our children played on the swings, lawns, and rocks of the sea.
They climbed the same trees I enjoyed at their age.
We fished the same waters around Sheldon Jackson rocks for coho.

I feel I owe Sheldon Jackson for the good life I've had.

At our recent reunion I was blessed to see Monte, Twilla, Edward,
Opal,
Fred, Ruth, Nancy, Marilyn and the original cast of 1950's SJ
graduates.
The varied lives they've lived with such distinction takes my breath
away.
I grew up where I was planted and have been happy for it.
My dad was right when he said, "Martin, Sitka has everything a man
could
Ever need or want."

FOUNDERS, CLASS OF '57

Often wondering about the Founders of Sheldon Jackson
I tried to put a face with a name so I could see.
I never saw the man, Sheldon Jackson, but he must have
Been serious about everything he did.
He must have carried proudly the name of Founder.

With so much activity going on in the formation of
The school a blur of faces comes to view.
Keeping the campus going like a clock and
Things mechanical one of the Founders should
Have been much like Charles Stuart.

Feeding the huddled masses with gourmet food
On a daily basis, with sudden deadlines
And an ever--growing chore list,
A Founder surely should have had the talents
Of a Jessie Frazier in the kitchen.

In my own life I've seen people in leadership at SJS.
They take their duty with a sense of dedication
And a forward--looking vision to life and us all.
When it comes to commitment to a cause
I think Roland Wurster surely has a place.

The people of the"Cottages" gave that sparkle to
The Founders eye in ever growing numbers.
Indulge me in my own grandparents lives where
Ralph and Elsie Young knew what a Founder could be.
By their example I am here today.

I see a successful hunter coming in from the woods.
His 25-20 Winchester lever action between his hands.
And bracing on his back a huge buck sways.
Providing for his family and the campus
I see Les Yaw the complete man and a Founder.

At the age of 15 she was a maid at Goddard Hot Springs.
Sheldon Jackson was a real moving part of her life.
The student store she managed for several years.
She sings the School Song with enthusiasm as she'll do tonight.
Florence Donnelly is a Founder in her own right.

In 1947 I laughed and cheered the Gilbert & Sullivan operetta
HMS Pinafore, a totally Sheldon Jackson production.
The complete Gladys Whitmore costume wardrobe was put to use.
Herb and Polly Didrickson made the Founders yell "encore!"
I was twelve at the time, sitting with my sister Sofia and mother.

Missionary to Gamble and Savoonga, Eleanor Rupert
Served in the early days of Sheldon Jackson School
With a great deal of happiness and pride.
Recently we see a reflection of a Founder
In the life of Angela Thompson.

It is not so difficult any more to envision what a Founder might
Look like with so vast a host of witnesses and so
Nearby you could reach out and touch one.
That is what makes this day so special today and over the years.
I stand in praise of Founders Past, Present, and Future.

SHELDON JACKSON HISTORY

In the creative clutter of my computer room I rise.
Insistent memories gather around me as I think of SJS.
It's as if I rise to gather strength, cranking up the boiler room.
Threatening redline gauges flashing on and off as steam increases.
The heat travels underground to the rest of the school.

Early morning girls make their way to Jessie's kitchen.
Their sleepy eyes quicken in the cold of a winter morning.
At last the dining room bells ring out and waiters do their work
Teachers full of expectation eye their charges hopefully.
Sheldon Jackson school is awake in warmth and purpose.

The Chapel speakers add to our lives their point of view.
Words to live by flow freely and catch an occasional ear.
Our world moves up a notch as we drift into thought.
Those lucky enough to be in the choir sing out.
We are what our Elders dreamed we could become.

She speaks of Egypt while teaching geology and we listen.
Her full life reveals itself in so many impressive way.
Vertical stripes in black and white our referee blows the whistle.
It, as usual, was a fair call but a really close one.
Basketball is a way of life here at SJS and its allure continues.

I carved a yellow cedar book end at the shop.
"Prayer Changes Things" is the message revealed.
The shop teacher looks pleased at my work I gave to mother.
My sister pages through the "Moonlight Sonata" before her.
Little did I know that she would soon perform it with skill.

My Hoonah side, Gerry, jumps high over the bar and hits the
sawdust.
Cousin Roscoe sails high over the bar at pole vault.
Kenny passes the ball to "Butter" who confidently makes the point.
"Starch" in white shirt ran over to visit "Fat Boy" in the crowd.
"Field Day" each spring was a community must--see event.

It is a quiet afternoon and the girls are sewing at Home Ec.
Making their own clothes and gifts for their friends was going on.
A sensitive teacher speaks as the girls think of their dreams.
The mission of SJC is moving forward with each passing day.
The swing at Stevenson rocks back and forth with boy and girl.

Sitting just a few rows back we watched "Pinafore" unfold.
Such beautiful clothes and the music inspiring tonight.
Later "Mikado," Nankie Po would steal the show outright.
The Whitmore wardrobe room was worth its weight in gold.
We listened as children to wonderful words and music.

REUNION 2007

Memories of the Past and surely the Present awakened in my life.
The gathering of my soul--mates for the weekend lifted my heart.
The flowering reality of Heaven blossomed and surrounded me.
It is as if the hand of the Divine reached down with tremendous
blessing.
The lives of those long gone quickened and mingled among us.

We, in unity, with smiles, tears, and purpose reached out to one
another.
Finding ourselves renewed and living together as in school days.
Kindled ancient echoes of our earlier lives wrapped in warmth of
friendship.
For a brief time we gathered in the peaceful beauty of our school.
Sheldon Jackson came alive giving us strength for our Future.

A TIME FOR SHARING

It is the night before the gallery showing of my work.
I found a richness in the work, returning to the past.
Faces spark my memory and names magically re-appear.
The campus comes alive to tell me a story.
Listening with my eyes and mind I remember happiness.

I am young again seeing the original setting crescent.
My grandparents intense dedication, tribe and church
Rekindles the special music of the life at that time.
Flying my first paper airplanes on the lawn as a boy.
Sledding down the hill when we used to have snow.

People are so amazed when wild birds land on the lawn.
They have done it from the beginning and still do it.
Ducks, geese, and shorebirds by the thousands came.
I walked the beach to school with my sister.
Marching forward our life was a life of the seasons.

Track sports on field days in the spring gladdened
Our young hearts as well as basketball in the evening.
Starting out as a photographer in 1960 in town,
Never realizing how important my work would come,
Decades later as I look over pictures today.

I seem to touch the lives of those long gone from here.
Their happy smiles live frozen forever.
My aunt Harriet Max with my tribal aunt Flora
Williams reflected much better days.
George Prescott grins from his old car as if yesterday.

Allen auditorium was the center of our universe.
The entertainment SJS offered was wholesome to all.
My mother, dad, sister and brother loved it.
To watch HMS Pinafore on a winter night was best.
As alumni we will gather together again in May.

FOUNDER'S DAY 2007

Founder's Day 2007: it seems like yesterday I was on the high side of
the campus.
My PBY glider smelled of fresh tester glue and rapid dry paint.
My brother John Bayshore helped me put it together for first flight.
In my haste to fly it I nearly tripped into the pole vault trough.
It flew gracefully down the green grass hill landing at the low tide
mark.

Rev. Webster recalled the days of Sheldon Jackson, the man.
There was a sincere reverence in the way he spoke that day.
How he started the school where he traveled in Alaska.
His mission to bring education to all Alaskans.
At the Allen building the crowd listened intently.

Sofia with her brown pigtails and I with my sailor hat
Ran to the campus to watch "Field Day" activities.
That day our cousin, Rosco Max Jr. was high man pole vaulting.
Another time Dennis Demmert was champion runner.
Gerry Gray did quite well at the high jump.

President "Army" Armstrong spoke fondly of the Founders.
The SJS choir sang "The Halls of Sheldon Jackson" with great feeling.
Cy Peck Jr. and I made the bass section sound good.
My sister, Sofia, at the piano winked to my mother and dad.
Andrew Wanamaker looked pleased at our efforts.

Well before sunrise Jessie Fraiser and her girls did magic.
They created treats with flour, dried milk and sugar.
The SJ lunch was always special, today included roast deer.
The Fraser hall boys also got clams for the dinner.
Throughout the seasons the SJS boat harvested game.

My parents decided to have me go to school there.
After high school at Sitka High, I enrolled at SJJC.
I lived on campus at Whitmore Hall facing the Commons.
Rex McKinney was my roommate at that time.
Among my chores was boiler room morning duties.

My favorite Founder's Day is always my NEXT one.
I have seen so many and had a part in several.
The passing parade of so many friends is well remembered.
The School has given me so many blessings.
So I spend my remaining time giving back what I've taken.

BURSTING WITH PRIDE

There was a time when my fear and dreams
collided sharply.
Holding on to my dreams for Sheldon
Jackson and fear that someday soon the doors
would close.
The rich tradition gone forever is an
unsettling thought.
Fortunately, those days are gone as the
school moves forward.
We have a working body of a well--oiled machine.
I visit the campus often with intense
memories of where we have been and a sense
of where we are going.
Thoughtfully walking the sidewalks I watch
Allen rise.

It is where I first took to the stage at the age of 14.
A monologue, "Man and the Mosquito," was a
humorous story.
With my mentor, Mary Prescott, standing in the wings.
I memorized it in detail with appropriate
gestures.
The release date was around Thanksgiving
In those days we had hunting and fishing
staff and ministers,
Reverends Arthur Bily, Elwood Hunter, and Bill Gavin.
The school kitchen was helped with fish
and game.

Also always doing his part was hunter, Les Yaw.
He gave the most inspirational devotion at Rotary.
Rev. Patrick Sheahan gave us an historic
View of Thanksgiving.
And also his personal view of his hunting
experience.

I am so glad that history has repeated
itself so often at
Sheldon Jackson over the decades of my life.
This gathering is blessed with good living as I look around the
room filled with dedicated, caring
teachers and staff.
I am proud of what is happening at my school.

WITH SUMMER WIND BLOWING

Endless memories swirl in my mind of the early days.
People surround my thoughts on a bright campus morning.
Looking beyond the gray day our thoughts hopeful.
Elders cheered us on our way to the living school.
Missionary role models gather at chapel time.

Each day stronger than the last, we advance forward,
Learning things new from caring teachers alive with wisdom.
Tribal drums in the distance remind us from where we came.
Not forgotten we carry them with us always.
Our new path broadens as we grasp our mission.

A new thirst for excellence builds and finds a way.
Greeting each morning we meditate on the day.
Thinking through the discipline steps of our lives
We begin to see our future direction coming up quickly.
This is the life we were destined to live!

Missionary brown buildings become our learning home.
We all help the campus effort with our talents.
Firing up the boiler room with menacing steam and dials
Was difficult but not impossible for a young Martin.
So early in the morning things got going.

What is it about this place that draws my thoughts?
Is it my fellow learners gathering and struggling to get ahead?
Is it the beauty of the minds pulling hard together?
Is it the commitment of those that come from afar?
Lessons learned prepare us for the new world waiting.

We gather at Sheldon Jackson in the harvest of our lives tonight.
Warmed by the remembered years so long ago rekindled now.
The joy of rebuilding relationships important in earlier times.
It is as if we could hear those dinner bells ringing as if yesterday.
I hear the music long dormant of our beautiful choir singing.

BOATBUILDERS AWARDS

The sharp sun lines came to see us yesterday.
Signs of spring sprang up around the campus gloriously.
Alumni and Boatbuilders told those valuable stories.
My closest friends gather in a circle of praise,
Talking as if they never left SJS warmed us all!

Names, long dormant, reappeared as living moments.
The years faded away rapidly and we were there.
Special teachers touched our minds and hearts.
Loved ones were full of greetings from the past.
Even the silent times expressed what words could not.

Hexagon chapel binds us with closeness unreal.
The man made Indian River flows beneath our feet.
Crystal clear water glistens in purity.
Our thoughts move upstream to valley and snow peaks.
The gifts of Nature continue to give their best.

To think of the lives so well spent in this place.
Followers of "The Way" showed what a meaningful life
Could be with love, care, and hard work.
A factory making lives the best that they could be.
Calling on us to share the new enlightenment.

How we depended on travel by the sea!
Such care in putting together the wooden boats.
Intricate details followed disciplined rituals.
We learned well and carried the lesson here.
The boating journey still continues to today.

Rich with detail, the narrators painted a picture.
Each with conviction walked us through the boat building.

The gathered wisdom of these sharp minds shines.
Humor broadened our understanding of the times.
I think we will walk tall from what we heard.

Those who deeply loved SJS spoke of troubling times.
They spoke of our glorious past and the people.
To make a future for us all we must talk together.
Full of expectation they wanted mutual solutions.
Later offering a prayer for healing.

The evening was ever expanding among friends
Those behind the scenes were praised for their work.
It was such a grand Tribal dinner!
Awards were given to Boatbuilders and helpers.
What an evening so complete with beautiful lives.

SHELDON JACKSON BOAT BUILDING HERITAGE

Henry Benson	Karl Cook	Joe Demmert
Herb Didrickson	Polly Didrickson	Laurence Doig
Cyril George	Gil Gunderson	George Haldane
Betty Haws	Andrew Hope	George Howard
Clarence Jackson	Ivan Jackson	Lawrence Jackson
Charlie Jackson Sr.	Mark Jacobs	John James
Samuel Johnson	Herman Kitka	Bud Lang
Louis Minard	Fred Olsen	Opal Olsen
Joe Ozawa	Louis Pazar	Peter Simpson
Peter Sing	Walter Soboleff	Verne Swanson
Raphael Towne	Gil Truitt	Ed Verney
Ron Williams	Leo Woods	Les Yaw
Bill Zeiger		Kathy Ruddy

ALUMNI OF SHELDON JACKSON

Mysteries of past lives were revealed since we left Sheldon Jackson.
Stories triumphant for those that walked this path.
Unfolding beauty in the lifestyles we chose breathed strong.
The people that made a difference in our lives lingered in our minds.
We are the survivors of the 1950's and beyond.

There was no small talk just true spirited men and women.
As the morning continued we saw clues more clearly.
The smiles were quickly remembered as well as the humor.
The story leaves little to the imagination laced with reality.
Our minds building ancient scenarios long dormant.

Coming together as we did leads to the importance of our mission.
Keep the school alive and growing for our children.
We have the spark to keep things going toward hope.
We are few but just enough to carry our message.
The school song lingering foremost on our lips.

The spirit of meditation that I learned here brightened.
There is a power for being part of this journey.
My teacher mentors marched before my mind as we spoke.
Whitmore, Gavin, Prescott, Robinson and Biggens rose up.
I owe the school so much and I will help.

I was pleased with the impressive lives that are here today.
Our varied skills tell of lives well spent and spending.
Reconnecting years of absence came easily and proudly.
We had lunch together and deepened the closeness.
The sense of caring people brought inner sunshine.

We'll gather at church with our rich cultural spirit.
At the picnic I'll remember our early food gathering,
Taking what Nature gave with deer, seal, berries and fish.
This is what we hold dear and enjoy.
The young SJS hunters heading out to gather food.

Remembering who was the best high jumper and runner.
The evolution of the basketball team moving up.
"The Mikado" production and our own stars.

SUN--DRENCHED FRIDAY
ON CAMPUS

In expectation we gather for the alumni coming.
Parts of Indian River flow just outside our window.
Last year a steel head swam in the clear waters.
Robins on the lawn give spring a fresh look.
I remember clearly my school time in this place.

The ancient buildings have their own language.
They speak to us in silent remembrance.
The times remembered shine in our minds brightly.
Thoughts of people come forward, who were here.
Teachers, staff, and students fill our thoughts.

Gone are the fun "field days" of yesteryear.
Our sporting skills were on display for the town.
Who will pole vault over 14 feet this year?
Rosco "Sunny" Max is favored to clear that height.
Herby will defend his long jump title.
Down by the sea is expert, Henry Silook; his sling shot sings.

The great lawn manicured to perfection is green.
Lovers walk hand in hand like Frank and Rose.
Blocking out the sun are thousands of shorebirds.
Herring spawning for a hundred miles.
Sheldon Jackson alive with activity.

Today in blossoming vitality we see the fruits.
Alert, confident students listen and learn.
The inheritors of history make their way.
In some ways alien to us, their knowledge spreads.
Their future reach is what we alumni praise.

The early vision reaches out, further, and finds us.
Some culture, some Western ways combine.
Today we take the best of all worlds.
Struggling to keep the school open is our task.
Our mission statement must not be threatened.

What can we do to make the school more secure?
The alumni face needs to be seen more often.
To help in any way we can is our goal.
Sparks of hope sparkle and help us on our way.
Willingly we move forward with surer steps.

SHELDON JACKSON THIS DAY

The same glorious song my ancestors heard I heard today.
From the woods the spring robin sang in deep beauty.
The same steelhead trout moved in the waters.
Beneath this Chapel is the man--made water path.
Each day a memorial in joy for what happened here.

We carried the weight of the world for those we know.
Each one of them stamped in our memory.
They walked with us on our life's journey proudly.
Teacher, parent, friend gave us something worthwhile.
The ever growing impact of this school added to our life.

Attempting to shield us from an ever distracting world.
To give us a chance for a life that was meant to be.
Our disciplined teachers fought for our attention
Hoping we would understand the importance of education.
We felt the urgency of their mission for us.

Those that have moved on we gather in memorial.
Very much a part of the fabric of our lives.
Last night we looked into our eyes and spoke of them.
The power of remembrance vibrated throughout the crowd.
Light--hearted moments were recalled joyously.

My decades of hope living for this school was spoken.
The need to remember the history of each life.
Near tearful but in happiness we spoke their names.
Our united thoughts spring to life their meaning.
This school helped us form our very lifestyle.

Martin R. Strand

The lessons learned in Chapel gave us a running start.
The personal messages and the messengers sang a great song.
Chaplain Pat carries on this school tradition today.
We have known great sadness but also great joy.
Sheldon Jackson College today is alive for us to enjoy!

OVERSEEING YOUR VILLAGE

You've been given options for the good of your village.
Deeply caring teachers busy themselves opening doors.
You take detailed notes and smile in a learning way.
There is no question too large or too small.
You become comfortable expressing your point of view.

Strengthening your tribal ways as you grasp modern thoughts.
As the drum beats your heart's rhythm quickens.
Organizing your life takes on a new vision.
Sheldon Jackson brings on an ideal learning setting.
Your life blossoms with a new discipline shining.

You gather here for many of your personal reasons.
How you've come to this place becomes clear.
Someone heard of this program, mother, elder or mentor.
You took the challenge, and are better for it.
Sometimes we must take risks to pull ahead.

You will take with you a new confidence about living.
Concepts learned will circle in your head as an understanding.
Your willingness to speak and be heard will move forward.
Taking your place in your village does not seem so distant.
We are pulling for your success in this venture.

Your village waits for you with your new found skill.
Their hope and expectations run as an incoming tide.
Elders nod their heads in approval as you return home.
Your loved ones feel something good has happened to you.
The new you sparkles brightly with new wisdom.

MY HOPE FOR YOU

Students in science and culture come to Sitka each summer and I took part in the program. The Answer Camp Assignment. There is a power in gathering talented instructors for the ANSWER camp of 2007. I was pleased to take part in this valuable institution. A Monday in July I did my one man show of poetry, juggling, and balancing act. For good measure I did my famous birds' songs. For the closing ceremonies I wrote "My Hope For You." Due to a schedule mixup I did not attend but leader Alfreda Jones read my poem and gave each of the 77 students a copy. Before she read the poem she asked the students "What do you know about Martin Strand?" A dozen hands came up outlining my various talents. July 22, 2007

Looking down on this special crowd I recall my early school life.
I never had much trouble speaking to an audience such as this.

I figured I had something to say so I might as well say it.
I never thought I had to ask permission to be successful.
It is my hope that you will go forward today with that thought.

I envision growing minds full of hope for their future as I look at you.
Some of you will leave your village to contribute to a growing world.
Others will be like me and yearn to go home and help your people.
The world will come to your doorstep with many great offers.
You will make a decision on how best you will spend your life.

I hope you will want to be excellent in everything you will do.
My elders and church urged my sister and me to be the best we could.
Our large and small victories were lavishly praised by them.
We worked on expanding our talents in many and varied ways.
I carry those talents with me today and use them often.

You let me into your lives with youthful gladness,
Thinking young again gives my life a needed lift.
Being so close to the future I see the good with what you are doing.
There is the promise of building your lives the right way.
The Elders here reach out to give you the beauty of their lives.
My wooden whistles have a very short life but fun for the moment.
The sling (shot) is made for recreation and hunting.
My words are there to let you know about what I have done.
My music would tell another story of the depth of my feelings.
Together I hope they are helpful giving you empowerment.

Today I praise this program you are involved in, expanding your life.
The teachers and friends are ever growing closer to each other.
Build on to these memories in the coming years ahead.
They will lift your spirits in the times when you really need them.
I know our Sitka, our Alaska, and our Nation will thank you.

FOOTPRINTS TO THE FUTURE

Soon you will be turning your hopes into dreams
And those dreams eventually into your reality.
You have taken many of those steps already.
Sheldon Jackson College had its part in your life.
This Baccalaureate will be part of your thinking.

Your footprints will work their way far into the future.
You'll look back and realize what you've accomplished.
The halls of Sheldon Jackson and Sitka will follow where ever you go.
Those who skillfully instructed you will be remembered.
And as alumni you will work to help the school.

In his academic world James Vanderloos related a comment to Justin
Tenzler who passed the words to Victoria Spencer who wasted no
time telling Ashley Saupe to contact Bill Payton that Angela Neilson
was heard to say to Gena Levandusky that Katy Ann Kelly cheerfully
passed the news to Karissa Hauck who in turn called Liesel Harvester
when ready met Emmy Garnish leaving no doubt to Cherissa Evanoff
to tell Teresa Bittler about their Associate Degrees.

While this was happening Rebecca Wells in cap and gown pulled
aside Sonya Weihl relating an earlier happening in which Joe Triplett
told Sheree Taki to get the word to Jay Swenson the pool player in
order that Kristine Swearingen might put a bee in the bonnet of
Sarah Stauber who laughingly pulled aside Monica Phle who ran
over to Jenna McGraw who readily told Amy McEntire playing pool
then slipped a note to Salomi Martin and John Martin that Tamera
Loveday a remark made by Erin Keenan quickly wasting no time
told the music maker Blayne Jessup who tooted his horn toward Ann
Hendry always ready to listen to let Tony Heerema know what Eric
Hannerman had said to Melissa Hamilton at the chapel filling in the
details to Bree (Jambor) Hack confronted Ryan Eklund to tell Matt

Dolkas that Denise DeGroot was willing to let Sean Conner give Cyndol Claycamp in so many words what Janet Cardenas leaked the news to Patricia Campbell finally told Evylyn Barr that Baccalaureate is the greatest event that ever happened.

AASJ VICE PRESIDENT SPEAKS

Like salmon returning to their mother stream we gather.
Sheldon Jackson is renewed again in our lives.
All the beauty of this place comes alive today.
Early remembrances embrace our thoughts here.
For some of us this was a true beginning.

I look to the stairs and recall teachers in my memory.
Struggling with my lessons I soon found my way.
Giving confidence was one of their gifts.
My Elders praised every advancement in my life.
This was our cutting edge looking to the modern world.
On a cold November night we sled down Stuart Hill.
Our ride takes us past the museum in a sudden turn.
The child, Martin Strand, shoots past our first church.
Scooting over Lincoln Street, we slide down to the flume.
It's low tide and on the ice our sleds continue 150 yards on the beach.

The center of our work and play is the campus.
In 1956 I travel to Philadelphia for General Assembly.
Elinor Matters is our chaperon on the long train ride.
We also practice the "Messiah" for the Christmas Program.
Music is one of the highlights of SJS.

Young men bring deer and other game to the SJS kitchen.
Jessie Fraser gathers the girls for Thanksgiving dinner.
They prepare the finest dinner I have ever had.
Later we gather at Allen Auditorium for a special program.
I recite "To a Waterfowl" by Willliam Cullen Bryant.

Today we gather with hope and anticipation for our School.
A lot of love flows from the past to the present.
We are pulling forward in our special memories.
A new day dawning around this school.
We alumni are witnesses to the Good Sheldon Jackson.

VISIT THE SPIRIT

In my own lifetime great women have served our church.
Sunday morning babysitters of Stevenson Hall when I was 2 years
old.
They were there for Sunday School for me when I was old enough.
Visiting missionaries from around the world came here.
New followers of The Way lived in the "Cottages."

This morning I visited the memories of those that served as well.
The Sunday School teachers, the choir directors, and motivators.
Georgia Conley, steadfast teacher and role model.
Gladys Whitmore, beacon of knowledge and strong faith.
Jessie Frazer, sparkling kitchen director and great cool.

Mary Prescott, brilliant orator and my mentor.
Powerful prayers in times of need by Edith Latta.
Organizational skills in the life of Wanada Holic.
Dependable service award goes to Euginia Williams.
Elinor Rupert off to serve Gamble and Savoonga.

Elsie Young's home on Kelly Street for women's meetings.
Evangelistic outreach of our own Julia David.
My aunt, Harriet Max, shining example of what a life could be.
Women of the Manse, Elinore Gavin and Elinore Hunter.
Elizabeth Peratrovich, civil rights innovator.

Organist Hopewell Rands served for many years.
Pianist and mother, Lila Newell Strand, most inspirational.
The good humor and sincerity of Lizzy Basco.
Pillar of the church, Martha Kitka.
The artistry and devotion of Esther Littlefield.

Today we pour all the positive imaging into the life of
the women who are dedicated and serve our church.

THE BATTLE

Sheldon Jackson closed this year. My heart bled at its passing. I wrote this poem for the last Volunteers in Mission group. I had coffee with them during morning and afternoon breaks.

During the battle I hid on the sidelines not taking any chances.
The Crusade took a crashing blow and I was not there.
Lives were lost and hurting, helmets and armor pierced and dented.
I pretended to be dead and the Evil passed me by.
Now I carry the guilt, knowing I did nothing to stop the bleeding.

You'll have to carry the news back to your loved ones.
That little church in Pennsylvania who gave and prayed for us.
Missionaries who faithfully gave of their resources monthly.
The Midwest corn states that kept Sheldon Jackson alive.
West Coast tithers full of hope with our mission.

Riding the sea of uncertainty we must move forward to survive.
As the hope of our ancestors we have to carry the torch.
The presenters of The Way around the Nation listen and wait.
We gather our thoughts on what to do beginning today.
Our hand reaches out wanting to help those in the trenches.

Our lives forever changed, begging for answers.
Give us a new day, oh Great Spirit, to face these uncharted waters.
We stand willing to help bring about positive ways.
Give me a chance to once again walk proud the halls of SJC
We hope this heavy responsibility will come to pass.

MONTE AND HELEN

It has been troubling being in the trenches in Sitka at SJC. I wrote this poem for the Volunteers In Mission who were the last to serve on campus. I met with them daily until the end at the usual coffee times. I know you contributed heavily to the school over the years and I thank you both.

Our reunion was so good and no hint of the coming ending was there at the time. The disappointment of our alumni is wide spread throughout the region.

The morning awakened as I sadly thought of the passing parade.
The church across the street was opened by the shaggy dog owner.
The long history of Sheldon Jackson people working closed.
The thought of the interruption of its mission was terrifying.
We, the cultural converted, bled with a new sadness today.

'Elegy of the Soul of a School' was my piano thought.
In the quiet of the church I played on relevantly.
Music the reflection of my feelings flowed off the walls.
Thinking of the hurt and bleeding spirits in a minor key.
The sudden adjustments of lives in the gathering crises.
I could feel their strength in the face of great difficulty.

Later I met with friends and I told them of my 'Elegy'.
They kindly asked, "Why not write about your feelings?"
Recalling the piano music I began writing in detail.
Remembering the sadness of the day I went forward.

Close to the grieving lives I wanted to somehow lift their lives.
To let them know caring people nearby were willing to help.
Working on taking away the dark thoughts was our goal.

They sing with their lives a grieving Requiem for the school.
The last of the summer soldiers coming from the West.
Many walks of life decades long in service to "The Way."
I, the sad watchman, see a splash of joy of their being here.
They answered the call coming without complaint to serve.

The birds and trees notice their coming.
Our fish and flowers feel the love that they bring.
The rising and falling sea crash against the shore.
On this cloudless, windless day we collect our heavy hearts.
The school has done so much good to lives around the Nation.

So valuable is their help we shed a hidden tear quietly.
They have left secure lives bringing a sense of adventure.
Our church bells feel the urge to toll with absent bells.
Our admiration runs deep from the beginning ancestors.
We feel the love of a passing parade of missionaries.

Our "Lacrimosa" is sung with pride yet in its sadness,
We sing hoping things that take time will solve.
Our historic choir remembers where we came from.
Our small band gathers and huddles close with sympathy.
Taking a well deserved break of afternoon nourishment.

These are some of my thoughts expressed to the Volunteers In Mission
who I got to know quite well over time. Historically the "Lascrimosa"
Mozart and a few of his friends sang together at Mozart's death bed.
It is particularly moving in my life as the Sheldon Jackson Choir sang
it under the direction of Paul Biggins so long ago.

CHAPTER 4   COMMUNITY RELATIONSHIPS

REFLECTIVE TIMES

July 11, 2006

Billowing clouds of discontent gather on the horizon.
My small life gets smaller, less important than before.
The joy of living lessons as I try to understand what is happening.
Alone we stand, not knowing the coming future.
Ignored by some but cherished by others is where we are.

The complexity of life weaves a strange tale going nowhere.
The willingness to forgive is there hopeful of a restart.
But who is to be forgiven? Who is the most wronged?
What really matters, today?

Bonds that were forged in strength slipping away.
Time goes on letting us know that time is short.
Where is the peace maker when needed most?
Waiting for something to develop is slow and painful.
The new day shows little difference.

Longing for the richness of life again is important.
My life force suffers ever reaching out for help;
My music tells me to be patient in a minor key.
How long away is happiness in our lives?
When will the daily tension lessen?

Putting on a happy face to those around me is getting old.
I gather in the security of keeping up an image.
Questions, pointed questions of others reveal our fate.
They are closing in on, perhaps, the real truth.
A delicate balance of what can be "aired."

In the meantime I go about my business hopefully.
I see the good around me in what I have to offer.
I will hunt my deer and catch my fish with confidence.
I will photograph beautiful images at sunrise.
And at dusk I will reflect on the good I have done.

NEW YEAR

Lengthening, the shadows of winter meet my gaze.
A holiday candy slowly dissolves in my mouth.
Remnant of those happier times begone.
Little of the season's cold is here today.
The Green Christmas is well remembered.

I hear the rain not on the roof but under the car's wheels,
Lapped up by rubber and turned to mist.
People hurry-skurry somewhere on New Years Day.
"Piano Grand" on PBS was never greater.
I listened and longed to be a pianist.

How can I best start out the year ahead?
What improvement do I see in my life that might make a difference?
To listen more intently with my hearing loss?
To concentrate in works or play?

To things that matter in my life I should pay more attention.
I should take seriously each day of opportunity.
I need journals for activities and creativity in my life.
I've tried to use only one journal for everything.
The problem is how to keep it with me.

My health is the strongest part of me.
A dry, hacking cough, perhaps from medication,
Is my only concern at this time.
My abs are flabby and I need to get rid of them.
More walks up Indian River are desperately needed.

My sling shot arm developed a soreness.
I think I can exercise it away and out.
It is my right arm so I tried my left arm.
It works but is less skillful than my right.

WHERE TO, NOW ?

Reaching deep into myself it is time for me to take a deep look into where I am going. It is the time of year I analyze the things I've done significantly in the year 2003.

It was a year of presentations in public for me. I read original poetry at several events at Sheldon Jackson, Blatchley School, ANB, Senior Center, and memorial speeches around town. For the most part they were well accepted and in some cases with no public reaction. Sometime I wonder if what I do is really necessary. I think it helps the community to have something prepared for every happening. I need only a little time to put something together.

Usually in the morning of the event I go to my computer room and compose something while listening to great music which really helps. I am the only one in the community who takes the initiative to present something timely in poetic meter. I hope it is viewed as something good as a written event commemorating someone or doings going on in town.

My commitment to Community Band is strong. I have missed very few practices and look forward to it each Tuesday evening at 7 P. M. My other tuba player, Elise, is really sharp and has had a lot of experience with other bands in her life. I am a bit of a showman and get the main solos for my part. She blends in well with the band and is also a good sight reader. Our band of 15 or 20 is excellent and growing in skill. We had our Christmas concert December 7th at the church and it went well. Also at the ANB Christmas party we played everything we had and the crowd was impressed.

Over the summer and fall I have been involved with Dog Point Fish Camp and this has been a deep commitment for me which I love to do. Earlier I shot a seal in the adjoining bay. My 223 full metal jacket bullet found its heart as it was on a rock and never left. We dressed it out on the spot on a cold rainy day with fall wind blowing.

I was at camp four different times this year and I hope my contributions were appreciated by the staff. I also did some reading of my work from time to time. I had many opportunities to sight in my guns and work up loads for hunting. This keeps me sharp in riflery and the good reasons to be a hunter.

JANUARY MOURNING

We are less for what has happened.
The gathering place for our minds slipped away.
The smoke was heavy and the damage vast.
The empty shell lies silent with no light.
Oh! The memories linger on this cold day.

The welcoming place in a happier time,
Where laughter echoed off the walls.
Our planning time for the day taken away.
Gathering our spirits we go elsewhere.
Seeking to be connected once again.

We talked of fishing times off the Cape.
Discussed hunting skills at great length.
Reluctant deer make their way to the beach.
Green Christmases keep the deer up the hills.
Sharing our lives with each other on those days.

Swedish pancakes smothered with strawberries
Fueled our thoughts and bellies on those days.
Heated talk about the way the town is going.
Save like a conservative but spend like a liberal.
We pitched in our own points of view.

Waitresses keep the coffee with whipped cream going.
Jim has to leave for work on the boat.
Kurt is flying out to scale timber in Kake.
Don is flying south for some quail hunting.
Martin is writing a timely poem for tonight.

Victoria's sooty, and quiet today.
Our expectations are high that it will reopen.
It has been a gathering place for decades.
It had other names with other people.
But it means something to our town.

Alone at my writing my mind reaches ahead.
Still seeking to be relevant in any way I can.
Living the life as an artist pent up in uptightness.
Legacy is on my mind and how important is it?
Have I given back enough to the life I have lived?

The emptiness of a distant family is heavily with me.
The time I should be sharing is taken away.
Listening to my serious music in melancholy of the moment
I hear the sadness of a minor key tugging at my heartstrings.
Who is left for me to give what I have?

What time I have left I should be constantly writing.
There is this urge to say something worthwhile.
I miss using words and music together to express myself.
They mean so much more when used together.
It is a reflection of a time I made a better contribution.

There will be a time when I cannot create and that frightens me.
A time when I will not care to be active as I have been.
I wonder how it will be when my mind slowly fails?
I see too many of my peers not making any contribution.
Perhaps, content just to show up for another day.

Right now I am pushing my talents to the forefront,
Knowing that I have to use and express them while I can.
I took an inventory of all the poetry I have committed to memory.
The list is growing smaller as each decade passes.
I find I must listen to deeper music before I forget it.

In the past I would whistle long passages of concert music.
I would sing in joy and sadness melodies remembered.
I miss my concert programs that enriched my living.
I want to memorize poetic works including my own.
Perhaps, I could record what I have written?

It is the end of the year 2005, my 70th year.
As is my custom I will write a fearless inventory of my life this year.
It is not without happiness and I have done many good things.
I feel the need to tell the story of my family while I still can.
Perhaps, this small laptop can contain in total my life story?

IN EAGLE RIVER

The planning considered in this adventure was light to say the least. I had no idea that the Christmas Camera TRADE Show was so poorly advertised. The extremely light turnout was disappointing to say the least. Only serious photographic minds were there and they got the savings that they needed. Few items were sold at face value. In my table all items got discounts when I saw the need to cut prices. I could have traded more with the other table owners. I did get two very good Miranda Cameras in a trade for my rare, Tower 35 mm and a 28 mm Takumar 2.8 lens. That was a good trade for me! I had to use every sales trick in the book to get the money I did get. It was around $460.00 plus small items.

Because I did not have a telephone contact I think I lost sales. I did give out several Postal addresses for my business but there has been no mail contact from potential customers as yet. I also listed Blondies Café as a meeting ground for intellectual camera collectors but no one took that seriously as of this writing. I am not giving up on camera sales. I will look for high visibility areas to show my wares. I have a lot of specialized equipment that a professional photographer would envy.

I will not let the pawn shop mentality get to me on this trip. There are other markets where I could move the stuff with more confidence.

It is interesting the new breeze our Indian politicians have taken with Shareholder relations. Just while I've been here I met with Johnny Hope, Richard Stitt, Carlton Smith, Frank Mercer and Ron Mallott. They have expressed a spectrum of potential action they are considering with shareholder interest in mind. I thanked them all for the generous $2000 dividend they so willingly gave. Some of them took the congratulations as the jest it was while others said that should have been more!

It was quite simply comfortable weather that greeted me on my first arrival here. Now we have zero degrees and lower. The usual cold ears and face are a problem from time to time. I am so used to dressing lightly that this is different to me! I long for the usual 40 degrees of

Sitka. I could use a long kayak trip of several days up the straights for deer! It looks like I'll have another "fruitless" hunting season this time around.

There are times I would like to do photography along the bus route. I like the frosted birch trees and snowy scenes. Last week I photographed a young antlered moose from the bus near Muldoon. The talkative bus driver alerted us and even slowed down and let me do my camera business on a sunny day. I don't have many results from my new Miranda cameras yet. I have one roll of 400 ISO loaded that I hope to have processed soon. It will be a wide variety of scenes from the bus and downtown.

Marcia and I have taken in two exciting movies. "The Rookie" with Clint 'Dirty Harry' Eastwood and "Sheen" was action packed with just the right amount of macho violence! Then last night we took in "Dances with Wolves." That was a siouxper! It showed a way of life that few today have realized. Academy Award material without a doubt!

Only one "bumber" incident so far. I bought a small new--looking tripod at the Salvation Army Thrift Store. I pulled out the legs and checked it when I bought it. However, when I got home I found that the third leg was glued badly and of course it broke! The risks I have to take, fortunately was only $3.50 so you can bet I will be more careful from now on.

I keep having hope that ptarmigan will show up somewhere here. I like to hunt this fine eating bird. I hunted with my brother, John Bashsore, in 1947 behind Totem Park. Hundreds of them came that cold winter. I have a Ruger Model lll 22 rifle here and I'll ask around to find out where they hang out this winter!

My shoes were totally unfit for winter weather of Anchorage. The black leather boots have no grabbing tread so I bought a pair that did. It is a joy to walk in confidence on ice and snow. I just hope they last until spring. Zero degrees and lower here and warming to fifteen above tomorrow.

It is always difficult for me to come into a 'hostile' emotional climate like what I stumbled into. Family values that were taken for granted or completely ignored have planted their seeds in discontent. Such is the scene at Eagle River. I've tried to keep an open mind about things happening but the prejudiced view I have needs a conservative hearing! I will always not understand the necessity for improving behavior through chemistry.

Some people think this escapist route will give others the message that they need help. Nothing could be further from the truth. Self hurt is so strong in taking this worthless path. The revolt against authority need not be suicidal to get attention. Communication or "let's talk this through" can really help someone in need.

What does freedom really mean? Is it following the wishes of Society with responsibility? Is it "doing your own thing?" Is it getting away from authority figures? I was appalled when the Berlin Wall came down. It was because of the wrong reason perhaps. My first impression of this sudden move toward freedom was met with a gasp, "Now we will have more people drinking and using drugs!"

Life should be a steady improvement away from things that are harmful to us and our children. We don't put our children into situations with bad role models for potential abuse. The positive sides of life must be present for good learning atmospheres. We have always promoted Freedom with responsibility.

Now that our children are grown up we take on the advocacy of good living from now into the future. Our effect might be minimal but our hope is maximal. Keep down the bad moves where ever possible! Start listening to survival instincts that lead your life into something meaningful for yourself and Tribe. Education always helps but can be expensive. We have to pay for the worthwhile things in life so it is a small price to pay to improve your mind and thinking. We will always promote education as a building block in life.

I'm not looking for family improvement as a record of my life but as a continuing goal in the collective lives of this family! I know that you all will have your contributions to the betterment of mankind in your own way. Please look for ways to help others in your area to look for higher goals. This will also propel your life to a higher plain. Please keep the communication connection strong within the total family. We will try to write, talk, phone, fax and keep information coming where it is needed and desired.

GRASPING THE CLIFF'S EDGE

The telling signs of advancement are all around me tonight.
My face sharpened against the blowing wind from Southwest.
'Clear days ahead' is the wind's meaning to me.
Bar-Tailed-Godwits are back but there are fewer than last year.
They are the largest of our shore birds heading North.

Short billed Dowitchers complement the Godwit's flight.
A safe rock surrounded by water just off shore they land.
Wary eagles focus their sharp eyes at these new travelers.
If they launch from their perch lesser birds take to the sky.
An uneasy truce is declared while skillful preening takes place.

They gather at the Turnaround behind True Value.
This vantage point is not by a long shot new.
It's the Kaagwaantaan stream from Swan Lake that brings food.
Dog salmon used to come here by the thousands in early days.
The flocks of birds carry on centuries old rest and feeding.

I have watched this beauty event for most of my life.
The visitors are a welcome change to the seasons.
They have a life and they carry it North to nesting grounds.
Lead by Nature they fly for thousands of miles to here, then there.
I note their visit and add to my bird life list spanning decades.

Would that I could ask them questions about their journey.
What changes have they seen during their life?
What does it take to survive the damage man has done?
Do you forgive easily or do you carry a grudge?
We share this planet and I wish we took better care of these creatures.

In 1994 I was the only one to notice the robins did not return.
I grieved that winter, wondering what had happened.
Fortunately, they came back the next season and I was glad.
Now I wonder about the Old Squaw ducks and the fur seal.
No more fur seal in the winter and fewer Old Squaw ducks in the
spring.

VIGIL DEEP INTO THE NIGHT

March 26, 2004

My devotional watching during the night with thoughts of Mother.
Healing from her loss so many decades ago is still here.
The vigil tonight is my connection to her spirit.
She slipped away during the night and I was not here.
I sang a sad song in this stairwell and felt better.

Music is the most spiritual side of my life.
The rich, colorful minor key is heavy with beauty.
In addition to sadness it asks questions of life itself.
It strengthens the sometimes lonely walk of grieving.
It helps in healing ways and brightens our way.

This hospital surrounded with sadness and yet much joy.
Many spent their first days and some their last.
Caring staff walk on that difficult road and do their best.
Relive the pain for another day and another.
They are such a blessing in our time of need.

My keyboard takes on a new life once again.
New themes are brought forward in the echoing walls,
Maybe others have had my burden and can understand.
The music is so personal to my life therapy.
Always reaching, searching for answers not far away.

SEARHC doctors, nurses, emergency crews and others
Serve us well with confidence and good humor.
In my own hospital journeys I thank them often for my health.
They have seen my public smiles and my private tears.
I come here tonight in praise of all the good that has happened.

SUMMER AND EARLY FALL OF 1995

After a thrilling time in Anchorage and Eagle River with Lila, Benny,
Martina, and Dennis we returned to Sitka to a triumphant welcome.

Sitka was its usual self-confident minus the Timber Dollars. The
realty people are in denial about what's happening in Sitka. Their
rates are way up and apparently won't come down in the near future.
The beautiful weather attracts record amounts of tourists and that
part seems okay. I lost my business by not keeping in touch with
them this season. I restored most of my own equipment and it is good
practice if business should come my way. Marcia got her dorm job
back and she applies the same dedication and care for the students.
We have a new mayor, Pete Hallgren, who was city attorney years ago
and kept up with city business by being on the Assembly. There were
quite a few running this year but I won't talk of losers. We kept Roy
Bailey, our Indian, on the School Board. The proposition # 2 was 50-
50 and the re--count was 50-50 until someone found 4 more votes for
the Yes side. It was about whether we should clear cut logs near Sitka.
Now the city doesn't have to promote that.
Kaagwaantaan (Kogwanton) brothers and sisters formed an
organization down at the ANB Hall. We will promote good tribal
living and dance. I joined, which is amazing considering my fractured
view of the culture. I plan to be a good Kaagwaantaan for the rest
of my life. We helped the following weekend with the Albert Davis
Memorial Funeral. I can think of no better choir music than was
sung at St. Michael's Cathedral that day! It reminded me of my early
days at the "cottages" when we would entertain Orthodox people at
Christmas and Easter. Our speaker for the Kaagwaantaan is Herman
Kitka. Ed Mercer is helping out in the organization.
Years ago I saw an article in the Sheldon Jackson <u>Verstovian</u> about
my mother's 8th grade graduation. Well, I went to SJ and copied it for
you. It's called "The Legend." It's something close to all of us and it is
a story told around campfires way back in time.

Concerning my guns I have to make some adjustments to the right with my rifle. When it was finished it was one inch high at 12 o'clock at 100 yards. The best shooting I've done in years! Before that I was content with three inch groups at 50 yards with my long barreled Smith & Wesson .44 magnum. I load for both guns and I put my reloading equipment to good use. I have been collecting it for years and it's paying off. Soon I'll be hunting in our good Easy Rider Kayak. I got it repaired this year and took it out two weeks ago.

Remember, we took it to Blue Lake and we all got in it!

The Greater Sitka Pool League is starting up again and I'll be involved. I was voted the Most Valuable Player last year with a tournament average of .934 wins. I could do no wrong! I have several extra pool cues if anyone wants one. Let me know what weight you need. We are using Valley National 8-Ball League rules and will be sanctioned this time.

Alaska Day is upon us! It's hitting Sitka hard this year with tremendous activities all this week (October 16th today) The weather is clearing but it might rain on Alaska Day the 18th. On Alaska Day in 1983 we visited Hoonah with the Daltons. Something happened last week that brought to mind our visit. Jessie talked about Sea Pigeons, which is a sub clan over there. Well, right after a storm around October 1st, I saw small birds flying around the harbor. I knew instantly they were Sea Pigeons! Their name was later changed to the western culture name of Sea Petral. Some of Martha and Buster's relatives are Sea Pigeons.

Recently, I borrowed a CD player and have been recording on my reel-to-reel recorded music from the library's CD collection. It is the greatest quality I have ever heard! I record 180 minutes per reel. The house is filled with Prokofiev, Shostakovich, Brahms, Beethoven, Yo Yo Ma, Saralsate and others.

Smoochie Annahootzy is enjoying himself. But he was a bad cat last week when he made his escape to under the house. It was late that night when we missed him. I took the air horn under the house and gave him a blast and he was very happy to escape back into the house.

Martin R. Strand

CHRISTMAS 1998

Eagles and Ravens
Frogs and Kaagwaantaan
German and Norwegian
Tlingit

Sara Joy is playing in the snow with Meta.
Martina called Karen over.
Martin Jr. takes a motorcycle ride with Dad.
Mother is making Christmas goodies.

We went up to the swamp and got a tree.
Bull Pine is so fragrant. Yellow Cedar bows perfume the house.
Uncle John stops by and picks up each child.
Christmas cards from Arlene and Marcus and other Grundy Center,
Iowa folk.
The church choir sings at our door and we let them in.
407 Sawmill was never so happy!

The new Salvation Army building is just completed.
The Karrases are our next door neighbors.
We gather together and head to the church.
Christmas Eve Candle Light service is good.

PART OF MY LIFE RETURNS HOME

July 27, 2000

Milling crowd of familiar faces long unseen brighten my way.
Sharpening memories, dormant but not distant, gather around me.
People that had important parts in the formation of my life are here.
Assignments remembered and well taught speak from my past.
Duet, "Out of the night that covers me" cried out tonight.

Lives well spent and spending like returning salmon beckon.
I thought of them often and find that they thought of me.
Smiles return from decades ago, lift our spirits gladly.
The boat heads out into our life's journey full of care.
Familiar land and sea marks pass as if in a parade.

Many a happy tear appears as we learn about our adventures.
We sadly learn of those who did not make it here and left early.
We will miss beautiful Betty K. and embrace her brothers fondly.
A nearly windless sea before us guides the boat across the Sound.
We make connections long broken and brighten with the news.

1954 State Basketball Champions are here and relive those days.
The Band members sparkle full of memories of Festivals.
Destinies flower in distant places but bring us Home.
Many made a difference in our world in helpful ways.
Some of us grew up where we were planted.

Stories of twists of fate in our work places are revealed.
Loving relationships that stood the test of time.
Grandparents focus on the beauty of their lives.
The legacy of children and grandchildren are the most special.
We made the most of our world as best we could.

The more we gather the more complete our lives become.
I look forward to widening our circle in so many ways.
The dream of the reunion became reality for me.
And I don't think I'm alone in these thoughts.
A wink, a smile, a nod verifies the truth of this gathering.

THE BOAT RIDE OUT OF TOWN

August 13, 2001

Like a military operation we loaded ourselves aboard ship.
Shortly after 11 A.M. we slowly backed away from the dock.
A brilliant sun helped us on our way out of the harbor.
Pioneers and Senior Center people and guests were on our way.
Seagulls took flight as we invaded their territory.

Seeing all the fishing boats docked reminded me of the past.
The boat "Muriel" looked like the old "Armour."
My dad, John Strand, leased from Russian Joe Skarus.
It brought back memories of my early fishing days with Dad.
30 miles off--shore we would catch 40-50 pound King salmon.

I was a small boy when the Naval Base was built in the 1940's.
My father had a part in the construction as did other Sitkans.
He and other carpenters and laborers got government paychecks.
It meant a new wealth and standard of living for our area.
I look and remember all the changes that took place here.

Our new breakwater we slowly passed by with birds ahead.
Mt. Edgecumbe in sun drenched glory looms large to the West.
A light Westerly wind means a full day of good weather.
Sandy Beach has crowds gathering to enjoy the water.
Halibut Point picnic area is full of fun seekers.

Hump backed salmon jump straight up all along the way.
They are still silver and making their joyous way to the streams.
Old Sitka rock brings moments in the past of coho fishing.
Starrgaven Bay alive with fish waiting for rain to go up stream.
Mosquito Cove quietly comes into view and one of our new trails.

Katlian Bay reminds me of my early hunting deer days.
Right after logging we had great hunting in the cut--off areas.
I shot four deer at 400 yards with my 264 Browning up the draw.
It was winter and it took half an hour to get to them.
I grabbed two and my brother two and we slid down the snow.

The middle stream saw Larry Anderson and I fishing for dollies.
A bear, bristling across from me, saw my twenty trout.
I warned Larry about it and ran to the boat 300 yards south.
I looked to retreat and saw a single sapling 100 yards away.
Backing in the tree's direction I made my get-a-way safely.

Our boat gave us a chance to renew old acquaintances.
People I grew up with, my peers, were everywhere.
We had a grand lunch packed by Senior Center workers.
My mind was re-living my past with Katlian Bay over the years.
What a treat from Allen Marine Tours on this bright day.

A FAIR CHANCE

For a long time justice was allowed to look the other way.
Lives discounted and thrown away without second thoughts.
Elders longing to give their grandchildren future hope.
A system so hostile wishing to replace the First Citizens.
We had done nothing wrong.

Tribal justice that was in place for centuries cut down.
Still positive imaging of the Elders managed to live.
They remembered and carried the good system in their minds.
The young were urged to learn Western ways and when they
Have learned they could protect us later.

There were others that saw that we were treated unfairly.
We were not alone for long, and help was on the way.
In the land we were born we could not own land.
Word of a Tlingit gold mine had to be held in secret.
A helpful missionary opened doors so tightly closed.

Evolving feathers of justice were beginning to grow.
Indian communities had their Elders speak in early years.
Brotherhood and Sisterhood flourished rapidly.
Monday meetings lasted till early Tuesday in deliberation.
Who will lead our way in these troubling times?

Elizabeth and Roy Peratrovich knew what was happening in the
villages.
They also wanted to own their own home in Juneau.
Disappointment met their every effort and they were discouraged.
How can we change the direction of the Territory?
We must alert the people of the Territory of these problems.

Opportunity presented itself at the Legislature for Elizabeth.
Her courageous words turned the tide of prejudice as we knew it.
Doors were opened for the betterment of the people.
Word spread quickly to ANB and ANS of this new victory.
Grateful Elders held Elizabeth in the highest esteem.

We still praise Elizabeth and those that moved us forward today.
A long list of those who encouraged her to step forward in 1945.
One of the goals of our Founding Fathers and Mothers was realized.
Our current Elders beam with joy seeing school children celebrate
today.
Elizabeth Peratrovich Day is for everyone in our State!

CAFÉ RACER

"Breathe Easy" for the day brightens to the touch.
That lonely muffin needs a friend.
"Orders to go are for sissies!"
Take the precious time to enjoy each other.
Internal sunshine always brightens.

"The mists hang low on the mountains
Like a guillotine over a condemned man."
This attitude is not shared by the regulars.
We share our fate with Nature.
While the Seasons nurture us with good.

Slowly I drank Snow Monkey Plum Tea from
Xanadu while the Mad Greek laughs.
Cars are racing by, some with purpose, others not.
Pleasant company moves my way.
I didn't know I could smile so well!

At Crescent lawn two horses move toward me.
Led by more beauty than I could imagine
I froze their warm gaze with my camera.
A passing cloud darkens against the sky.
My bike moves confidently forward happily.

A Highliner greeting ready to serve
Takes my breath away!
Jena foams exotic flavored whipped cream
Into my cup and all's well at two bells!

I live a recycled life.
I collect from those who have upgraded.
This computer pre-loved by someone,
Sings well to my touch.
Polished White E shoes step lively.

MY LIFE'S OPEN WINDOW

January 16, 2003

The Library door opens just a little after 10 and I am let in.
Opening of opportunities somewhat strange to my mind's eye.
If I had a lonely thought it is quickly diluted in the rooms of
knowledge.
In the silence I seek blossoms to beautiful poetic music on the printed
page.
1620 original verse is so much a part of today.

I am greeted as a poet by a caring librarian on her busy day.
Mime children talking to mother through sound proof glass glisten.
Some days the click of Internet keyboards swells in volume through
the room.
Such energy communicating to others far away as one could imagine.
Perhaps, I shall join them down the road freely chatting.

Earlier at the "Great Book Sale" I buy hundreds of dollars worth of
reading.
"Pet Loads" by Ken Waters looks at first a dog and cat primer.
It is the most valuable tool for the ammunition reloader.
$46.00 each for volume 1 and 2 from hunter Dagwood Mathews of
Sitka.
I take my prize home for only $1.00 each and develop new loads for
hunting.

Summer music festival artists' music I take home as rare diamonds.
I relive the concerts of last summer in the deluxe CD collection.
The Pacific Coast Service of Radio Moscow on short wave in 1944
Began my quest for great Russian music played between propaganda.
35 years later I find the music I wanted by Lowenthall with orchestra.

A tap on my back while reading reveals a smiling close friend.
Muted exciting talk begins and has to be continued outdoors.
While sitting on the benches a fishing seal comes into the harbor.
Yellowed and red leaves mark our path back to the warm room.
Such an ideal place to meet friends and gather in the highest
thoughts.

Here poetry is held in such high reverence the old books are never on
sale.
For years this policy puzzled me and was a source of disappointment.
Over the years I have followed the Sitka libraries since the Tower
Apartments.
Enriching my life, and that of my family I still come here.
Reaching out for knowledge and a little happiness.

SILENCE AS NO LONGER GOLDEN

January 19, 2004

Sitka silence was no longer golden regarding civil rights.
The people of 1964 gathered together to show their support.
President Johnson signing the Act to become law of the land.
Alaskans were no strangers to what was going on in the nation.
We gathered at Sheldon Jackson for the famous march.

People of all walks of life stood up and walked proudly forward.
I was a witness on the sidelines but showed my support.
My camera spoke of the cause of freedom unfolding before me.
I felt the richness of the day in my darkroom processing.
The music of Beethoven echoed as I printed the pictures.

Keeping ahead of the crowd with my bike as they marched.
Down Lincoln Street people gathered, cheering us on.
The church and American Street were in my images.
They carried signs and flags as they marched.
I'm told a small band of hecklers jeered from the sidelines.

Business men and women, teachers, fisher people, moved silently.
The sun brightly shining on this special event.
Children also took part in the parade with their families.
Looking at the pictures today I remember many of their names.
Dr. Martin Luther King was held in high esteem for his work.

I have met people that have worked and marched with him.
He was a powerful role model for all of us.
Taken long before his time was a cause of deep sadness.
His work is remembered with reverence and continues.
My heart is brightened to see this program today.

With programs of remembrance like today keep the dream alive.
As I write this morning I listen to a C minor symphony of Beethoven.
I feel deeply the struggle Dr. King fought so bravely while here.
I hear the heroic cause that he gave us to complete.
May the Great Spirit bring sunshine into your life.

A LUNCH TO BE REMEMBERED

May 22, 2004

The song of their lives brings us happiness.
Such willingness to serve brightens our day.
There is music and strength to what they do for us.
At 11:30 I see our help coming up the stairs.
Shining faces give our lives such a lift.

Norman swiftly whisks them into position.
With military caring precision they gather at the ready.
Exciting salads are served with such grace.
The bread and milk children move swiftly to the crowd.
Eagerly we lean forward waiting for the main event.

We've seen the menu for the month and today.
The cooks and servers are poised for action.
Table # 1 leans forward in expectation.
The chicken royal is served quickly to all.
The children look surprised when I mention their folks.

Sometimes I remember their parents and grandparents.
The beauty of their Sitka lives recalls an ancient echo.
We elderly care deeply about their growing lives.
What a good start for their future life.
"Would you like this dessert?" A young voice asks.

We see them in music concerts and sports about town.
We see them down town shopping at the holidays.
At the playgrounds they notice us and say, "Hi!"
We are a community of caring, sensitive people.
Thankful for this very special kind of help.

FOURTH OF JULY
2005

With all our freedom on this sacred day we rise.
Our hearts beaming a light into our past.
Many nations do not have the freedom we have.
Our footprint fades away in the mind and sand.
But the strength of our collective lives remains strong.

We rejoice with the families tonight in fireworks!
Generations before us have shot guns into the air.
Our children lit sparklers and firecrackers around us.
In my day cherry bombs, roman candles and rockets burst.
Lighting the skies with many beautiful colors.

July 3rd, 1943, my father, John Strand bought fireworks!
His father Martinus and brothers caught 14, 000 pounds of salmon.
Dad spent $100.00 worth of fireworks for us.
Our neighbors in the"cottages" helped us fire them.
It took glorious hours to light them all to our joy.

Years later in my teens Hammy and I found a cannon.
It was a 10 gauge Winchester with wheels.
We staked it down above Indian River and fired 25 blasts.
The high brass shotgun ammunition had black powder.
With each firing a thick black smoke filled the area.

Tradition has it in Sitka that on the third of July
We would fire our guns into the air at night for the 4th.
Shotguns, pistols, rifles and even flare guns opened fire.
And those who could afford it, they had sky rockets.
It was a real salute to the freedom we now enjoyed.

Today we watch the fireworks across the world.
In every time zone on TV we watch in wonder.
Our thoughts are heavy with our fighting forces.
We carry on our traditions hoping for their safe return.
The work of Freedom continues every day.

ONE HUNDRED AND FIFTEEN YEARS AND COUNTING

An ancient lady dressed in black warmed herself on the beach.
It is said that she was near 100 years old.
We children passed by her on our way to play in the water.
Totem Park, as we called it, was our favorite playground.
In all seasons we would gather in the forest and the seaside.

John Strand, my father, and I in the row boat fished for coho.
We would hand troll near the flats and caught many
Coho before we reached Indian River. I was six years old.
Shorebirds by the thousands sang their songs in full volume.
The sky darkened when they took flight heading North.

World War Two came to Sitka and machine guns in the Park.
The mouth of Indian River was dredged for gravel.
The replica blockhouse beach had ponds thirty feet deep.
When the tide went out fish were trapped for good fishing.
Herring, trout, salmon were caught in their season.

Warships and amphibian planes anchored close to shore.
Our young minds were filled with wonder at the sight.
Patriotic Tlingits signed up for the service of their choice.
We practiced blackouts and escapes to the forest.
Thousands of troops were in the islands and some in the park.

Soldiers and their girl friends walked "lovers lane."
The USO was busy with lots of local help.
My dad, John, helped construct Japonski Island buildings.
The Sitka economy was busy in ways that amazed us.
Military radio stations started up and we listened.

In August of 1965 the National Historic Park was completed.
It was my honor to photograph the ceremony.
I borrowed a Zeiss zoom lens for the event.
I pushed the film to a higher film speed to shoot inside.
The Tribal splendor was magnificent!

Totem Park was my Spring bird watching time.
My life list of birds increased with every passing year.
I still enjoy our flying visitors in their brief stop here.
When I was young I found tree snails near the fort site.
Sad to say I never saw them again.

Now I wheel my bike through the trails with memories.
I recall going over the bridge and seeing deer making their way.
The salmon in hundreds below me busily spawning.
Rough legged hawks flying full speed through the trees.
1947 ptarmigan by the hundreds came here from Canada.

My children constantly enjoyed life on the beach of the Park.
We learned to kayak riding in the waves to the shore.
The "cottages" people landed on the shore with game.
We dried herring eggs high in the trees for grandma.
Out on the rocks seaweed was drying in the sun.

We all enjoyed the Park in our own ways.
I read somewhere it is our Nation's smallest park.
But it will always be big in my family memory.
A happy 115 years for Totem Park and hoping many more.
It is a great therapy to restore our spirits again.

HONORING VETS

Over the decades we at the ANB Hall have seen the wars come and
go.
Our native warriors have fought for our country many times.
We early on realized freedom is not free and took a stand.
Protecting our people and Nation was always in the forefront.

Alaskans of every kind have served with distinction for our country.
We joined other groups in search for the common good.
We have sacrificed in the bloody wars and lost precious lives.
Advancing from fox holes to the hill to victory.

We gather here tonight to honor those who made the final sacrifice.
We remember them well on this day with sharp grief and love.
Flagging their graves our tears are filled with sad remembrances.
We marched today down our streets full of pride having known
them.

The Alaska Native Brotherhood welcomes you to this event.
We salute the caring people that put this evening together.
Thankful that the Sitka Community Band is here to perform
The music of marching times honoring those who served well.

SAD DAY AT 402

June 30, 2004

Clandestine trickery moves into our lives and is not welcome.
Trying to do the best we can is our main goal for today.
Internal emotional bleeding continues although we look okay.
Misunderstanding with a healthy dose of not caring is upon us.
We all want to do right but the results are really different.

Perceived steps toward authority is firmly in the mix.
Money power is winning when used as a weapon.
It brings up its ugly head in so many devious ways.
When used as a control tool it is very hard to address.
Those without lose everything without a fight.

Family drifting apart for the slightest of reasons.
A word here and action there with little explanation.
Trying our hardest to understand and not given the opportunity.
It comes out that we are the enemy without a trial.
What is the solution to bring things back to normal?

Must someone lose or can both with effort be winners?
There is so much to gain by working things out.
The awkwardness cannot continue and ruin everything.
What would be the ideal first step?
Where will this eventually lead?

THE COLORFUL MAN

(Impressions of students appeared in the Letter to the Editor, put together by Martin Strand, presented on March 17, 2006.)

Their assignment was to describe an important person.
They jumped into the project with enthusiasm.
This colorful man is big in the thoughts of our school.
In learning times and fun times we gather around him.
He is called "awesome" and "cool" in so many ways.

Dressed in black and on rainy days yellow, he is impressive.
He brings to our school a reasoned and bright image.
They feel he communicates well with each one of them,
A cheerful figure during our lunch time he joins us.

Sergeant Green lifts them up with his wisdom.
They feel they can talk to him in great detail.
One of the best parts of Officer Green is he listens.
Many said they feel safer when he is around.
Watching over our school is his real duty.

Reading the descriptive writing I have a sense of wonder.
The depth of their writing takes on surprising turns.
"He makes sure that nothing bad goes down" one said.
"Intelligent because he has to do stuff," another relates.
"He is a police officer and that is what I want to be."

Today we gather in praise of Sergeant Ed Green.
The classes of Ms. Janelle Favour have an ambitious project.
They have shown a good person with a sense of style.
Those of us on the sidelines cheer their great effort.
We join Blatchley Middle School in honoring Sgt. Ed Green!

OUR JOURNEY

This was written for the Archive department of Sitka Tribes of Alaska. I am a volunteer in this project and took a trip to Oklahoma in October of 2007

There was poetry in the way they moved full of purpose.
Their lifestyle was poetic in their thinking and their walking.
I now could see the artistry and oratory in their stories.
It was my wish that I could have recorded their voices.
My Tlingit grandparents are shining memories in my life.

All we have is somewhat crude audio recording of the past.
Some recorded at the slowest speed to stretch out the time.
At that speed the quality was poor at best for music and speech.
But it was a record of the times wanting to reach to the future.
Ancient Native dance and oratory recorded for our time.

It was not part of my world and I could have been a help.
I was building a life of my own and did not look ahead.
The older ones were getting older and leaving the scene.
How I lament the opportunities missed in recording them.
I look to these reel-to-reel tapes to do some good for us.

Not understanding the language I feel the rhythm and meter.
I feel the poetry of those recorded moments bringing a life.
I have pictures of those Elders that paved the way for us.
50 years and more are visually recorded with my camera.
My negatives still have a sharpness and brilliant quality.

Moving from one old format into the new is our task.
How long will these recordings last in the new medium?
When will the equipment become obsolete and die away?
Our future generations are depending on us to save them.
Do I have enough time to make a difference?

We are starting out on a soul searching journey soon.
Looking for the right answers to preserve what we have.
We seek some wisdom of other experts to reveal the truth.
We will lift up our lives with our own strength.
There are valuable moments to be recorded in our journey.

Am I ready to reach out for the help I desperately need?
I want to be responsible for bringing back something of value.
This is not a passing commitment and then moving on.
I will be called on to follow through with good planning.
This may be one of my most important jobs of my life!

NATIONAL CONFERENCE OF TRIBAL ARCHIVISTS

Libraries, and Museums, Oklahoma City.

Conference subjects include Past Perfect Museum software, Planning and Implementing Oral History Projects, Collection "Development for Tribal Libraries in the Electronic Age", and Role of Tribal Governments in Preserving Culture.

All aspects of interest will be discussed in detail by the presenters. In implementing our program to go forward. Subjects include: financial, best locations, equipment, good managers, great leaders, the challenges of Collections, from Idea to Reality, The Inside/Out View of protecting Collections, Digital media, Storytelling for the Modern Age.

We gathered united in multiple ways working toward an understanding of our "Lifeways." Instead of Lifeway we use the term "Life styles." Sensitive to the varied cultures here we spoke diplomatically for the broadest understanding. The crowd wore regalia of gold, silver, and rare stones made up the jewelry of the heavily beaded in Tribal glory. Faces full of character and beauty were everywhere with smiles to match. A strong sense of "Family" reaching to the ancients colored our ever--advancing outlook. There was a feeling of something very deep about being in Indian Country.

Our Sitka team soaked up the positive atmosphere happy to be here. There were other Alaskans in the audience as the conference pushed forward. Archivists, librarians and museum people of all Native races graced the scene. The press was ever nearby plying their trade trying to get to know us. They were a friendly lot wanting to learn more about our Lifeways.

It is in a deep, sense of appreciation that I took this gift of a trip with the blessing of Sitka Tribal Association. I might add that the background meeting here in Sitka with the museum and repository people and the State of Alaska curator, Sean Lanksbury, enabled our team to have a lively technical discussion on our goals at the conference. "Guardians of Language, Memory, and Lifeways" was the conference theme. We learned that Roby and I are "caretakers of old words." That is the root definition of an archivist. The words and dance on our recording tapes and other media carry our language and dance forward for future researchers and Tribal members.

Susan Feller, conference director, led me to the banquet head table for my part in the program. I was honored to sit with the Kiowa women when the master of ceremonies, Curtis Zulnigha, introduced me and I gave my Tlingit name, clan and house before giving my poem "Oklahoma Adventure." The banquet hall was filled with conference people with hardly a seat left.

OKLAHOMA ADVENTURE

With a Nation screaming for literacy I invade the life of librarians.
I, the egocentric broadcaster wordsmith, am taken aback in awe.
A peek into this other lifestyle I see and feel the beauty before me.
A life of determination and dedication shows its working face.
Caring, articulate museum people surround me with their high goals.

With lives sharply focused, intent on serving their people I feel as
Intruder, empty and longing to be filled with their kind of hope.
Listening intently with our group I am looking for new standards.
Inspiration in my learning ways builds with much appreciation.
Today, I am enriched and growing with so much caring help.

The rain--soaked bus rides into the morning strong with purpose.
Strangers become friends, talk across the aisles as smiles broaden.
I speak in good humor to my new neighbor about my life.
We pass two Native casinos and ancient urges sweep my mind.
This gamble of life has a partner out there blinking its light.

Then ganged up on us those experts in the field of helping others.
I reached into my college life pulling out what skills I could muster.
Alien after years of little study my mind unwinds of remembered
times.
When thinking was so sharp and work of the day so right for the
moment.
Poor is the Nation that has no heroes. Disgraceful are those who
forget.

I look to our Elders language for the future generations.
Preserving their writing and oratory is our task today.
Reel-to-reel voices of another time jump into our lives joyously.
Our ancient ancestors speak to us again trying to show us the way.
The research continues to bear fruit as our work moves forward.

Cinnamon sticks fuel our meeting into the night, brings us joy.
Learning our personal journeys we laugh and become closer.
Everything is working for our benefit and our eyes sparkle
Into the gathering night we move on to our resting places.
There is another morning of opportunity tomorrow for life!

ADA OKLAHOMA

With Gary and family, Halloween 2007

It's Halloween and ghosts are flying all around Gary Brooks.
He is sitting among his classmates listening to his grandpa Martin.
The stories keep coming about very friendly ghosts in his family.
Great, great grandma Dwee, Tlingit Kaagwaantaan (Kogwanton)
Flies into the room smiling at Gary although he has never seen her.
She remembers us all from our very beginning to the present.
Her village Angoon is in Southeast Alaska near Juneau the capitol.
Dressed in ancient red and black wool regalia and dances to drums.
The drum heart beat of the Tlingit Nation beats loudly as she sways.
Other members of the Tribe dance in increasing tempo into night.
Gary's eyes light up as the leader makes his entrance.
It is Koohuk the great, great grandfather looking pleased at Gary.
He carried a huge staff with totem designs that he created.
On his arm are heavy bracelets carved in silver and gold.
He is an expert Tlingit carver and presents to Gary a canoe.
It is in red cedar with a big Raven on the bow of the canoe.
Although Gary is somewhat afraid he takes the canoe gladly.

Gary's great grandmother, Lila Newell plays Chopin on the piano.
Her father John "Koohúk" Newell bought her the piano when she
was eight.
She loved the piano and gave her first public concert in Sitka at her
home.
She was one of the first Tlingits to go to college at Oregon State.
Pausing at the piano she looks at Gary and asks "What school is
this?"
"Willard and I could not be prouder" Gary answers in his quiet way.
"I feel you will be successful," great grandma Lila says with a wink.
Then she flew away at warp speed off into the night.

Grandpa Martin continues his story on this Halloween with some poetry.

CATS AND BIRDS

Seeing the winter birds come back lights my day.
Looking into my window the Evening Wren coaxes me to action.
The seed bin now empty and the seeds that have fallen are covered
with snow.
Turning its head to the side then the other it looks at me.
"Can't you tell a hungry bird sitting on your tree?" it urges.

Twenty--five pounds of bird food lays in the cold hall.
Big seeds, small seeds, and black seeds, which are their favorites?
Three plastic tubes are filled and swing in the winter wind.
Half of the harvest spills to the ground by the time I put it up.
Sinking three inches into the soft snow the bunting cracks seeds.

Evil starlings linger near the feeder and I violently shake the blinds.
They fly away only to come back when I am gone.
The crows too heavy to peck the small feeder hole swing the feeder.
The Junko mine the snow beneath just as happy to find a meal.
The snow truck makes a racket and they disappear to the trees.

My cat used to sit for hours at the window, claws raking the glass.
While there I tried to pet him and got a menacing growl.
If it were an outdoor cat it most likely would be a hunter.
But now it is content to be detached intense actor.
Three Decembers ago Smoochie-de-Long left us for good.

People who love pets are good all-around people.
Pets are a life-long commitment for better or worse.
Sometimes in the night I feel my cat is somewhere near.
Blending in the dark shadows its spirit lingers.
All the love we had for it warms our lives in memory.

This Fall I went to Swan Lake to check on my Dragon Flies.
They were there and plentiful and I wished I had my camera.
As I walked near the duck feeding area a Greater Yellow Legs flew in.
This stilted shorebird made a landing thirty feet from me at the
water's edge.
Before it could settle down a small brown hawk grabbed it.

It was a sudden death and the hawk struggled with its large prey.
It set a course across the lake to the alders with much difficulty.
Flying like a butterfly just inches off the water it made it across.
What a meal that must have been as the sun was setting.
I gazed in amazement at what I had just seen.
In my early years working as a janitor at Mt. Edgecumbe
I came across a strange sight in one of the barracks on Alice Island.
I was to sweep an empty attic heavy with a light dust.
As I came to the one window I found large, brown, dead moths.
They were the size of humming birds and so unusual.

In the years that followed I have seen only a handful of those moths.
They fly with a low buzzing noise when they are near you.
The wings are rapidly moving somewhat like a humming bird.
I've heard them more often in darkness in Totem Park.
Louie Minard and I saw one at Bear Cove one summer day.

CHAPTER 5   MUSIC MAKES THE MAN

NOTES ON PRELUDE

My early dealings with the church was with music. Many people influenced me musically throughout my life. My mother. Lila Newell Strand played great music for me as a child.
The Sheldon Jackson Choir's songs of praise and joy inspired me to get involved with music. The early Christmas pageants of Sunday School brought out my dramatic side.
"Messiah" by Handel in the old church filled me with yearning to take part which I did. The Christmas duets of John and Wanada Holic made the holiday special. Xylophone music of Clarence Rands and Hopewell on the organ or piano played beautiful music. The focused dramatic singing of Mary Prescott was an inspiration. Most of the Sheldon Jackson staff contributed heavily to the music world of Sitka. Pageants, operetta, Christmas, Easter, and Thanksgiving programs the staff was ready and able to perform with confidence.

Soon I became involved with piano and tuba. I played tuba at Southeastern music festivals in solo and quartets getting many first ratings. I played solos at the church, "Asleep in the Deep", "He will hold me fast" and others. Later I became interested in piano compositions and variations which I composed the hard way, note by note. With my radio and TV involvement I used to play piano during the breaks between video tape changing by Harry Lanz. Harry would say, "I need two minutes of music" and I would play on the studio piano. I started recording myself with reel-to-reel tape recorders in the 70's and continue to the present. In 1990 I received my first Casio 625 keyboard and did some of the most creative music of my life. The thought of 200 voices at my command was mind boggling!

The music today represents a memorial to those mentioned earlier. It is a sad beauty in C# minor full of rich chords and variations. Remembering those gone on is often tearful but full of respect and joy for having known them. January 1996

DREAMS OF MARTIN STRAND FOR 1999 AND BEYOND

There is a need in my life for continued growth as a musical performer. I enjoy presenting something meaningful that shows something of my potential as a musician. It is true I am limited in musical literature but not in understanding the dramatic visual and performance aspects of a fine piece of art.

1998 saw me playing more around town, especially at the Lutheran church. I experimented with an ancient, restored organ. The most interesting times I've had were with the Yamaha Synthesizer with its many voices. It has a mode that sounds like a choir in chords and melody. I also play their piano. The people there sincerely enjoy what I do.

I do this because my own Kohler-Chambell piano is dying a slow and painful death after over 100 years. I miss the practice I had from 1985 to 1992 at my home. It was such a joy to behold but my ears were deaf to its terminal death. I could not hear it getting out of tune until 1994 when I realized I should have done something to save it. Virgil Hale, the blind piano tuner, first mentioned that the sounding board was cracked and could be repaired. He told me what to do and I did nothing.

The history of this piano blinded me and I only heard the beautiful chords that my mother must have heard when she first played it around 1913. I remember her playing by herself after she recovered from TB. She knew she needed the practice and inspiration it would provide. I often wondered about the ballroom dance music she played as a young woman. It must have been quite a sight to see this beautiful lady perform so elegantly around town and at Sheldon Jackson events.

The Tlingit community truly loved this part of Western culture because there was so much good in it. I look sadly on the closing of the Cottage Community hall in the 1920's. It had to do with missionary objection to the evil of ballroom dancing and music. I strongly believe that the love of music was the real reason the Alaska Native Brotherhood hall was built. It offered the natives freedom to grow and express ourselves in music.

And the ballroom music of the times was a positive force in many relationships at the time. The Salvation Army was growing in Southeast Alaska and along with this growth musical instruments were introduced in our Area. Sheldon Jackson School was also instrumental in realizing the high self esteem music brought to their students. Another aspect that is rarely discussed is the military service trained many Indian musicians who later returned to their homes with good musical talent.

The Cottage Band was quite good in the 1920s and there were other bands in Sitka at the time. Alfred Gordon was conductor for many years. The band would travel by boat to other communities and perform at ANB and ANS conventions. A noteworthy performance was in 1929 in Haines ANB Grand Camp. The band played three encores of the William Tell Overture to a thrilled crowd.

I remember my mother, Lila, and sister Sofia playing Primo and Secondo parts to the Poet and Peasant Overture by Von Suppe.

I think I turned pages for them and loved it. When my mother attended Oregon State she took an advanced piano course. I still have the 1924 piano course at home. The thing I noticed about the course was the intense attention to detail about the composer's lives in addition to the theory and practice of their music. I sometimes wonder where she would have gone musically if things were different. In the 1930's she turned ill with TB along with a large part of Sitka citizens. She was weak when she had me and when I was three I got TB. I was weak in illness for quite some time. It delayed my school and I entered the first grade at age 9. I was there for about three days and moved to second grade because I knew my ABC's and could count but that's another story.

My family always encouraged my sister and me to get involved in music. Sofia took to the piano early, very early and soon was performing in public at church doings. Grandparents Ralph and Elsie Young were pleased along with the entire Native community. My role at that time was to enjoy the music presented by my mother and sister in addition to beautiful church music at Sheldon Jackson.

Every church event had new and exciting musical performances and of course the songs we love to sing again and again. I'm still that way about music. So my dream is to build musical blocks and expand my talent as far as I can go.

What am I doing with music now? I have a love for ancient music makers. I have two reel-to-reel tape recorders. One by Akai and the other by Sony. I have always had a technical interest in recording. My motive was to get high quality recordings of poetry and music together. This is some of my enthusiasm for dramatic presentations. I had a Sunday afternoon poetry show called, "Words and Music."

It was extremely self--serving for me because it combined what I loved the most, drama! It started at Sheldon Jackson Junior College. This is where I was first introduced to hands--on radio. KSEW was my first major job and I hung out there amidst other talented voices. We each had our own agenda, but we worked as a team at that time. Preceding me at KSEW from Sheldon Jackson was Ray Paddock who later because President of Tlingit & Haida Central Council. He had a warmth about him that gave him quite a following.

Early on I took to Classical music and this means everything from Baroque, Romantic, and symphonic works. I studied the record jackets and the record company commentary and expanded my studies of music appreciation at Sheldon Jackson. Of course I had musical background from my mother and the church. I also expanded to production and did commercials and special events productions. I would play music new to me and read the detailed descriptions on the record jackets and learn while I listened. It was such a discovery for me to find out about so many wonderful and exciting musical compositions. Later I finished two years at SJJC and was to receive a scholarship at Ohio State University in Columbus, Ohio. The benefactor was Fred Palmer of Worthington, Ohio. Rolland Wurster, then president of SJJC, called me into the office and told me of this possibility. But it was Army Armstrong, president at SJJC that saw me off to Fred Palmer's.

ANB CHRISTMAS TIMES 1999

Like lightening it struck me, realizing my heritage.
The music of my youth comes back strong.
The powerful choir of the Native Church sings.
Taking me with them in meditation and rejoicing.
My grandmother, Elsie, turns and smiles seeing me
Singing at the top of my lungs.

That's all they ever wanted, giving us a fair start.
The growing distractions of the world were moving in.
"Buy our children time" they seemed to say.
Positive imaging so intense it was hard to refuse,
We followed their role model and stepped into a new world.

I look at the floor of the ANB Hall and wonder.
See the deep loving scratches of ballroom dancing.
See heavy dark shoes moving and carrying the
Dead for mourning here.
See the joy of voting rights at last is ours.
Dream of a better life to come.

Indians Newell and Young find gold north of Sitka.
Some good came of it.
We bought an education and we held expensive land in
Seattle for a while then bought a house for $2,000.
A piano for my mother, Lila, from her dad.
Oh! The music that rang through the house!

It's Christmas and we have no turkey.
From the kitchen wondrous smells come out.
Smoked deer meat and potatoes.
Three Entrance Bay Goose roast and goose tongue salad.
Blueberry and salmon berry pie completes dinner.
Gather around the piano with joyous songs.

The Sheldon Jackson Christmas program is next.
Students and community members join in and stand
For the "Hallelujah" chorus by Handel, sometimes sung
Twice, it was so good.
On December 5th of this year I felt that greatness
As I played tuba in the band and the Harry Jansen Choir sang.

Music has always been a powerful influence in my life.
I think it's the most spiritual thing I do.
It seems to grasp at good things we fail to express.
Another dimension of feeling that speaks to us.
For all the unexplained goodness I am thankful.

This brings us to tonight.
We call on the same strength as our tradition.
We struggle to keep our culture.
We sing of our victories.
We laugh in good humor.
Our togetherness unites us for another Christmas.

MUSICALLY ENHANCED

April 16, 1998

Coming from a musical family is the most helpful talent a
mother can give her children.
When I play the piano in memory of my mother I use the
richness and beauty of a minor key.
Music is the most spiritual aspect of my life.
It is the window to our soul and speaks loudly of our
Tribal family values.
The sadness and pain of losing someone you love can best
be expressed for me in the C# minor key.
I am talking to those gone on through memory enriched music.
When I heard the children sing and dance like the ancients
I sparkle once again with renewed hope for the future.

CASIO KEYBOARD OPTIONS 12-07-98

CONCERTO # 1   CHORD 'ON'.   RHYTHM = SWING.
Lower TONE - Preset A+Brass Ens....upper tone # 7
Tempo 30% ACCOMP 50 %.....rhythm off ..

CONCERTO # 2,   CHORD "ON"—RHYTHM = SLOW ROCK
LOWER TONE = A Preset + Brass ----Upper Tone = {reset AA=9
RHYTHM OFF =====ACCOMP 50%

CONCERTO # 3 CHORD 'ON' RHYTHM = SWING
LOWER TONE +A+ A===UPPER TONE PRE B + 8 + SELECT.
RHYTHM OFF. ACCOMP 50%

CONCERTO # 4   (Rest Ye Merry Gentlemen)
CHORD 'ON' ===RHYTHM = SLOW ROCK ----LOWER
TONE PRE A - VIBROPHONE (Brass) —UPPER TONE PRE A +
7 +
SELECT. TEMPO 30% ACCOMP 70%—rHY 50%
MAIN VOL MAX

WEDNESDAY IN REVERSE

2000

A delightful CD of music raises my spirit to a new high.
"Les Classiques du Classique" from France, of course.
J.S. Bach Partita #3 in raw beauty strings to my heart.
Victoria de los Angeles (soprano) with nightingale softness
Beats with delicate wings of song to me.

Tchaikovsky: Serenade for Strings (Moderato) speaks to me.
The Snow Maiden by Rimsky-Korsakov warms a cold image.
In my own prison I feel a strong freedom to live.
Sparked by fuel of my inherited blood I quicken.
I was meant to be musical and am moved deeply.

I would just as soon listen my life away in such company.
The music reflects on happiness, triumph, sadness, loss and finding
Elements of my life that have been and meant to be.
Windows to where I've been and with whom.
The music of Nature plucks on my being constantly.

I live each day from musical thought to thought.
From dire mood to full realization of my fate to come.
To acceptance of where I am with life, now.
Cleanse my mind of distractions and fill with joy.
Alone I face the future that opens new possibilities.

Herring eggs spiked with hemlock flavor I had for lunch.
A single taste takes me back 60 years for a look at
What a rich life I've lived and full of thanks am I.
I surround myself with people of vision and worth.
What I leave behind is up to time, the healer.

The bottom of the page I reach so soon when I want to write.
I miss my motorcycles and the freedom they gave.
Healthfully I now ride a fine bike to my future.
I miss my darkroom and the creativity it gave to me.
My pager rings perhaps from someone who cares.

TCHAIKOVSKY'S # 6 MONDAY

Adagio-Allegro non troppo from Symphony # 6 of Tchaikovsky
deepens my thoughts of myself. My heart beats to the sound of
mourning horns and muted drums and cello distant. Soon the slow,
melodic theme envelopes my total being.

I remember how things worked so well in the past. Everything I
touched turned to gold. My wishes were paid in advance. Just a
glance and journeys were begun and were completed immediately.

Then the wake-up call to 1996. My heart was 90% blocked and
needed attention. The first time I realized death was nearby. Alert
hospital people attended to my needs. The flight north, painless but
full of mystery.

The music charts my struggle to stay alive. The fears, the doubts, and
approaching the unknown. I had to do some serious thinking. I was
not ready to make any plans for the future. I guess I'd have to stand
on my record.

That was three years ago. Today I breathe easy and accept my sad
fate. Everything turned out fine. Pain and suffering held to a bare
minimum. I eat well, exercise by bike, and live from day to day.

The most important thing on my mind now is my will. Who will
want what I leave behind? Is my work worthy to my survivors? How
is a lifetime divided up fairly? Is it worth something to them?

Cameras with attitudes. Cameras for parts. Equipment ancient and
needing attention. Dying negatives and rejected prints. Imperfect
images like my life.

A computer room like a museum. Long obsolete computers and
printers. The collection of a recycler. Living well off what others cast
away, that will be my legacy.

My life is a work of art in progress. I will work on the bright colors.
The huge canvas on the ceiling. My strokes bright and clear.

There is travel on the horizon. There are places I've never been. What
would I miss if I leave? What is so important that I stay? Change is
certain and mystery the unknown.

Reflections in the mirror show long aged lines. My face distorted with time. Still I press forward in this I call life. Pain feels far away as it never happened.

Bike parts dying in the back yard. Cables rusted solid beyond repair. A porch that needs painting. Caving in shed roof droops. Razor grass grows high in the back yard.

Beyond wishing I don't move forward. Ambition long gone to me. Sad at the thought of not doing anything. I dream of a better day. I add garbage to another day.

The sea calls me almost daily. I want to explore places out there. I want to sleep on a quiet island. I want to fish for my breakfast. All these things are possible, some way.

The band plays on and I'm in it. The brightest hope of the past 40 years. I can play and I can learn! My dream has come at last!

SEARHC PRAYER VIGIL

It's been my privilege and honor to be part of the SEARHC Prayer Vigil over the years. I must admit it is mainly therapy for myself that drives me to play the music in the stairwell of the hospital. It is an evolutionary part of my early work as a janitor in Ruby Gossett's Army. Sound played an early part in my life as a musician and the stairwell bounced my voice in exciting ways. We had many beautiful choirs in the 1950's and I sang bass in the Sheldon Jackson choir. For years I wondered how I could connect with my mother who died at Mt. Edgecumbe hospital. Only a few years ago I came quite accidentally on a solution to my problem. The stairwell! This time I played my Casio Keyboard and it had such an effect on me I do this every two years. My C# minor "Meditation " is the most colorful piece I play with variations. Since music is the most spiritual thing I do, I now feel a connection to my mother who I did not have a chance to say goodbye to. I also dedicate the music to the memories of my grandparents, brother, mother, father, aunts, uncles cousins and many others.

Thank you SEARHC Hospital for the chance to express my grief and eventual triumph in such a special way.

NORWEGIAN RELATIVES

My first musical deadline is April 21st when the Sitka Community Band begins its Spring Concert. I've been working on my upper register of notes all the way to B flat. My technical practice books are extremely helpful. I can mark the fingerings and after a little practice I remember them. "Forty Fathoms" is coming along nicely. Section 3 needs concentrated work and a little faster. The finale has syncopation where timing is very important. "Norland Overture" has rapid high notes in cascading order that I must get right. My other tuba player, Elese does good work with her unblemished tuba.

For over a year I have been planning to recognize my Norwegian Relatives in a musical presentation at the Lutheran Church. Sunday that dream became reality. "Men of the Sea" I dreamed up to commemorate Martinus Strand and his boys John, Knute, and Kaore. Ample reference to Sophia Fredrika Dahl who married Martinus in Norway and traveled to America with the boys to settle in Tacoma. 5209 South Puget Sound Avenue was their home. In the summers the young men went to Alaska with Martinus to fish. "Men of the Sea" starts with rolling waves in a minor to C# minor and moves on to a Beethoven like introduction of the main theme. A (I thought) thrilling finale rounds out the piece.

The crowd sat patiently since it was the Postlude and gave good applause at its conclusion. I received quite a bit of thanks from the congregation as I exited the choir loft and down at the reception. It was a good move on my part to see it through to the end. Joyce and John Mac Donald sat in the choir loft with me during the performance. Note: I played the special music during the offering. I chose to use the synthesizer in the choir setting. As the Mac Donalds exited the choir loft with me several thought they sang the offering music. The choir setting sounds so human and was so effective.

THURSDAY MORNING WITH DAVID & MARTIN

Nothing is by chance on a radio station. This is the plan for the outline for an interview.

1. Interview with Martin Strand (David reads TW part and does introduction)

2. Music from Cassette from Martin. Original keyboard piece by Martin.

3. First poem

4. Eroica Trio doing Rachmaninov "Vocalise" 6:44 Track # 10

5. Second Poem by Martin

6. Mozart Symphony # 36 Track # 7 10:42

7. Poetry

8. Kachaturian Piano Concerto in D Flat Track # 2 Andante Con Anima

9. Alaska Native Brotherhood essay

10. Syrinx by Piatigorsky Track # 17 1:33 with Nathaniel Rosen cello

11. Tlingit & Haida report

12. Beethoven Piano Concerto # 4 Track 6 9:02

13. Improvisations

14. Prokoviev "Classical Symphony" Tracks 5,6,7,8 15 minutes

15. Beethoven "32 Variations for Piano in C Minor" Track 1 10:31

16 Closing

TECHNICAL HAZARDS

Clumps of sound discordant
Race to be heard in the faulty CD player.
I must remove the unit and save the music.
Swiss symphony never sounds this disjointed.
I tried to clean the CD player twice with no results.

Music is so important to my life.
It leads my mind into deep beautiful thoughts.
It directs my moments in heroic ways.
It helps me understand why I am writing.
New meaning built around who I really am.

I will never select the RANDOM mode to listen.
So many people do and it dilutes musical thoughts.
The symphony from beginning to end is the right way.
Several of my C D players for the computer have failed.
Perhaps, the power system is overworked.

I can hardly wait to have my 600 MHZ central processing unit.
Give me the additional power my system might need.
I have high hopes that it will smooth out in clarity the music.
Someday soon I will edit video media and add sound.
Production is my forte and it waits not so patiently.

Carefully I have put the motherboard into the case.
Hooking up the indicator lights was a problem for a while.
Finding the right 40 pin cable took three hours one night.
OH! The happiness at getting the hard drive to respond.
It was one of the highlights of my computer experience.

What will the future hold for me in my productions?
Will it come easily or will I be plagued with hardship?
The temporal life of a working computer is on the edge.
A lot of negative things could go wrong very fast.
I'm hoping to pull forward with my wit and wisdom.

My horn blows a sweet melody wanting to be heard.
The collection of my life's effort I will write in detail.
Composing something meaningful is my only goal.
Blossoming forward with the Spring light I see clearly.
Fruitful expression over a long period of time I want.

MUSIC JUXTAPOSITION

My sultry sounding synthesizer wails out a Far Eastern tune.
I don't know why I'm drawn toward this music.
It just appears in my mind and I am hopeless to stop it.
Easy for me to understand the rhythms of ancient music.
I sway to the beat to the exciting conclusion.

Opening my mind to tone possibilities is the keyboard.
The joy of creating something strange and new.
New options to this piano player increase my thirst.
Every voice suggests a mood, a rhythm, and song.
Now all I have to do is work on written notation.

I've progressed musically toward more dramatics lately.
Like life my musical moods change with the times.
The tragic beauty of a minor key full of color is displayed.
The rising crescendo adds meaning and texture to my work.
As I understand life more, my music is a reflection of it.

Listening to great concert music of the Masters guides my life.
So much variety and energy with deep expression fills me fully.
I'm still discovering music that might have an impact in my mind.
Gustov Mahler's symphonies have been a tremendous influence.
It takes time to listen and learn from a great composer.

If I could give some of this knowledge to my grandchildren!
Sometimes I feel so selfish keeping all this GOOD to myself.
The winds of change are blowing and soon I will burn my own CD's.
I will put together all the music that has meaning to me.
I have a life why not share it?

In an earlier time I would whistle whole passages of music.
As my hearing diminishes I've lost the upper hearing ranges.
I still whistle and try to test those upper ranges.
As I start out on a bike ride I often whistle from "Carmen."
As I race toward the park the "William Tell Overture"sings.

Music is constantly in my mind from waking to deep sleep.
There is always a sound track going on, whatever I do.
I would be nothing without my words and music.
This is how it is and how it shall be.

SEEING MYSELF MORE CLEARLY

December 4, 2001

Extended Tribal family have been ignored and are becoming distant.
Another Christmas and New Year is coming without entertaining
them.
Maybe, someday I will have a house to royally treat them.
That time is not coming very soon, unfortunately.
My name is not very large on their horizon.

Even more sad is my moving away from listening to great music.
Since my reel-to-reel tape recorder falters I have not listened.
Such a wealth of music I recorded from records and CD's.
It was a stable part of my life and living.
I still listen to CD's in a limited way.

I have opened my musical mind by being part of Community Band.
It is such a joy being part of something greater than myself.
I lament SJS and Mt. Edgecumbe giving up their music programs.
It would have been the key to a better life for the students.
I know what that life can be and it makes me stronger.

I'm still learning programs from my computer.
To be a more fully literate person has been one of my dreams.
I use perhaps 10% of the computer options but that is enough for me.
I'm growing more expressive of my feelings and surroundings.
It keeps my mind busy by urging me to challenge each new day.

As I write today, I listen to Mozart's "Ave Verum" which colors my
thoughts.
At Sheldon Jackson I sang with the choir several of the pieces.
It strikes a chord of harmony and conviction in my early life.
I am the product of the best of the missionary mind of the day.
Music explained so much about living the good life for me.

Early computers in the 1970's and 80's began what I'm doing today.
I used them for self analysis and therapy at the end of each year.
It was perhaps the most truthful part of the writing I did.
I have many of those early looks at myself and I notice similar traits.
Some of the same problems arose then as they do now.

Like a gathering of angels, "Ave Verum" sings a song of a better life.
The people of my old choir come to life as I listen intently.
The Indian church of my dream is shining in the Sunday morning
sun.
"Messiah" is remembered in exquisite detail as I sang bass.
Tonight I play the parts in Community Band on my tuba.

STILL MORE CLEARLY

December 4, 2001

Looking into my soul today I don't see what others have seen.
I see the strong idealist that I am, full of hope for my people.
I see my attempt to push myself forward in non-threatening ways.
I see my talents not used to full advantage or used at all.
I see myself as worthwhile and a contributor to the greater good.

Others may see me as light on commitment.
How does my track record play out in their minds?
I know that I am a late starter in group politics.
I am aware of what kind of impression I must make.
Perhaps, they think I don't need their approval.

I don't think my recent defeat at the polls is earth--shattering.
I can pick up the pieces and go forward in the level of commitment I
want.
It was my goal to give what I thought I could give comfortably.
The public may have caught on to this rationale.
A vote of 13 to my 11 indicates I have a well of support.

Indian politics is strange in so many ways.
I have fallen victim to it as I look over earlier times.
I lost being a delegate in the past one time at the flip of a coin.
You must pay your dues by showing up often.
Visibility at the right places really helps.

There are so many things I want to do, so I am relieved I lost.
I will find other creative ways in doing the work I want.
Writing, music, hunting and fishing need to be brought forward.
I'd like to plan 2002 with a sense of style in my life.
Video production is waiting in the wings and beckoning.

Before I lose the talent I must do something meaningful in
photography!
Dead and dying prints and negatives are everywhere!
There is a lot of good to be done with my images.
I dream of two years of printing long-forgotten negatives.
My cameras have bleeding batteries bent on destroying them from the
inside.

There are so many ways my life could go.
To be fruitful again seems so distant a dream.
Wanting to connect with my children in meaningful ways would be a
goal.
They will have my footprints in their lives when I'm gone.
If only I could give them what I don't have to give.

CANDLE IN THE DARK

July 8, 2004

Bela Bartok plays in my computer room as I think of the past few days.
His searching, compelling emotional music seemed just right for now.
It tells me of something newly missing that left on last night's plane.
The Anchorage bunch left carrying our hearts with them speeding into night.
Denali, Lila, Martina, and Dennis blessed our house with richness.

Our remaining crew bent on finishing touches brightens our day.
Our renewed house sparkles without clutter and waits for something better.
It tells us of dreams not yet dreamed of hope for a new life close by.
Sound echoes nicely from the smooth, painted walls willingly painted.
Chris, Neal, Martin Jr., Cherie Tyler, and Shelby are here!

Taking the kids to the playground yesterday was pure wonderment!
My frisbee arm slightly sore but feeling good after all that action.
Badminton rackets beat that bird over the swings over and over.
Seeing how their lives were going from just this short time.
I see lives of much activity and caring for each other and working lives.

Something I noticed at the church lunch needs attention.
I played the piano and the children came over to join me.
They took turns plucking the keys then Denali played.
She composed a piece and repeated it as I accompanied her.
She has the gift of music running in her veins, please explore it.

It was joy taking care of the lunches throughout your visiting us.
It was so rewarding seeing our house changing for the better.
Shostakovich Quartets warm my writing as the music changes.
The music guides my thoughts as many grandfathers before have
done.
I am a very wealthy man to have support of such a caring family.

Many hands have worked swiftly, without complaint, erecting living
space.
We benefit by their efforts and are full of praise for their having been
here.
Soon the last workers will be gone and we will be arranging the
rooms.
New priorities will advance our progress into the future.
The helping hands will always be remembered and appreciated in our
lives.

Step by step, moment by moment, improvements miraculously
appear.
Water-soaked and distorted ceiling tile are dashed to the floor.
I quickly gather them up, bag them and they are whisked away.
The staples that held them are removed professionally.
Ugly water marks on the ceiling are soon gone for good!

Dennis and Benny put 8 by 4 foot dry wall up and screw it in place.
As if by magic the room suddenly seems so much brighter.
I am so hopeful that things are on their way for the better.
Detailing on the panels are put in place and they are secure.
The house takes a giant leap forward as something wonderful
happens.

The talk continues on a high plane by the workers used to such
precision.
Figuring out where to cut for the best results, things are put in place.
Years of getting it right, Dennis instructs Benny to do the right
moves.

A symphony of activity falls into place that has its own music.
A keen sense of appreciation builds in the grandparents of 402.
It is time for lunch at the Alaska Native Studies lunchroom.

Director Dennis Demmert stops in with words of encouragement.
John Hughes, citizen of the year for Sitka, joins us for seconds.
Ribs with cole slaw salad is the main menu item.
I think of the time I spent at SJ as a young man learning.

Back to workplace and a few more hours of fruitful effort.
My dreams return and seem more possible with each passing hour.
I will be able to expand my horizons with this gift of space!
Yellowed with age wooden tile in the kitchen is taken away.
The dumpster fills for the fifth time and they come to get it.

The front door is taken down in its decrepit state never to return.
The new door jam is carefully placed and adjusted many times.
The door is put in and is fit to perfection and swings clear.
Martin and Neal busy themselves with the new paneling.
Dennis fills the ceiling with dry wall and leaves space for the light.

The ancient piano is witness to all this activity.
First tuned in 1932 by Dd. A. Sherif the piano turner of the day.
The piano bought with the first gold money from our mine in
Chichikof.

MUSICALLY RESTORED!

On Wednesdays we take a ride into our past.
Sometimes carefree and sometimes serious reflection.
Willingly we listen, hanging on every remembered phrase.
Humming along as salad is served and wanting more.

The music of the 20's, 30's, 40's and beyond fills our minds.
Of those times important and loving in memory.
She brings sheets with bird scratches like talking leaves.
The sound reaches deep into our lives as we listen.

Table # 1 hopelessly weeping tears of joy at the
Music reaching our eager ears and fills the room.
Burgeson tinkles the ivories to fulfilling climax.
The applause increases at the "The Sound of Music."

My spirit is lifted as "Memories" from "Cats"
Is played just as I remember watching the Broadway show.
Sue Burgeson plays the Senior Center piano for us
Each Wednesday thrilling our lives once again!

MARCH INTO THE FUTURE

I can imagine how it is to work toward peace in the world.
It would take a lot of hard work and challenge.
What is Sitka doing to move in that direction?
From what I gather, peace is much like music.

We have the makings of something wondrous.
Our lives mean something moving toward beauty.
Our machine is collective music bright and shining.
The language is music lighting our path.

We listen to each other and express our feelings.
Each Tuesday building into the next with expectation.
The degree of difficulty increases and we work it out.
Each one doing its part toward the finished product.

I struggle to fit in with the group of fine musicians.
Sometimes the ancient echo of my past musical life sparkles.
A rhythm, a phrase, dance in my mind with pleasure.
Community Band confidently supporting the melody.

We are moving on rapidly in the right direction.
Composers live again on the page before us.
Our working minds again lift our spirits.
Love blossoms like the coming Spring.

As a young man hunting with my dad on the cliffs of Verstovia, my
dad said, "Everything a man could want or need is in Sitka." In my
search for beauty and enlightenment over the years I find it in the
Sitka Community Band. It answers my question, "When at last will
my life ring true?"

RELATIONSHIP BLUES

The bucket of tears is overflowing with new purpose.
A strange emptiness erupts, carrying me with it.
Reaching into my past comes to haunt me.
Living over and over again my mistakes.
An overpowering light flashes a new kind of pain.

A terrible truth that a heart awakened to a great love
Is also opened to great pain.
Family fleeing away at light-year speed surrounds me.
The likelihood of coming back is so remote.
My life hanging in the balance by a thread.

Prokofief's "Symphony # 1" plays my feelings today.
Confused, depressed, is the musical treatment.
The building emotion of a people reflects sadness.
It is not without resolution or hope.
Movement toward solution it strongly suggests.

Some day, perhaps soon, communication will open.
Being the subject of such hatred is difficult.
How can the blame be equally spread?
Do I have the ownership of the blame?
Is there anything in my life worthwhile?

Prokofief suggests dialog in a constant stream.
He also suggests searching for answers.
It is such a dark side of life I see before me.
Perhaps, there is a path back to reality?
Listening suggests hard work ahead for me.

I get up in the morning and go about my business.
My bike defines my motor skills for another day.
Numeric meditation (cards) moves my mind.
I can relate to numbers as a problem solver.
Thank goodness I still have some friends.

AH, MUSIC

A new window into my world has happened at last.
I have recorded music that means something to me.
It is a journey I had very much hoped for most of my life.
I at last have the tools to do production long dormant.
If only I could express the happiness I feel at this moment.

My fairly ancient computer, which I put together in 2000 works!
600 megs of ram serves my 20 and 80 gigabyte hard drives.
This last week I struggled for the computer to recognize my second drive.
After a neat bit of sword play and guru' help it is possible.
Listening to a CD I recorded is the frosting on the cake.

It is mind boggling to realize the possibilities I have unearthed.
I have longed for creative production since 1977.
It was the year I left radio and TV and began a new life.
It is in my reach to open up my dreams that visit me.
My poetry will take up a new and wondrous attitude.

My first efforts are already underway.
It is a musical look into my dream to make a comeback!
I have steadily moved toward this moment for years.
I had to start to care about myself and life.
There is much to share about my experiences of worth.

It is no secret that I have a deep love of music.
Music formed my life from early childhood.
Mother Lila and sister Sofia played piano.
I listened intently and molded it into my life.
Their duets resonated in my mind almost daily.

My artistic side is heavily leaning toward written work.

I am trying to visit my early life and remember and write.
It is much like an ancient misty dream of uncertainty.
Picking up pieces of memory comes with difficultly.
I walk my early years over and over.

The exciting details are coming back slowly.
I walk to the Park picking up events of those times.
The sea gives me hints of where I have been.
The deep woods speak to me of good times.
It is all making sense in great ways!

MUSIC OF THEIR LIVES

Thinking of the spirit of my grandmother and mother.
Grandma Elsie and mother Lila bring to my mind reference.
It is the music of their lives that is with me still.
I remember the humming in the kitchen preparing dinner.
The hymns came alive with praise in our church.

Since music is the center of my most spiritual side I listen.
Uplifting concert music with great depth moves me.
I imagine the lives of those departed come alive again.
I am connected to the richness of a minor key.
As if they are giving me advice from afar.

The piano was the first Western influence in my family.
It came as a gift from our Sheldon Jackson teachers.
A whole world of expression was opened to us.
We embraced all that good music gave.
I am a product of those beginning musical times.

Another year of grieving is upon us today.
Family and loved ones have entered that deep sleep.
Our music takes a somber, reflective tone of sadness.
We gather closer together seeing answers in our pain.
Our church is here and our Elders speak to us.

The best of our Tribal ways hold up our lives.
The beauty of expression lifts our weary hearts.
We sing and beat the drum as in ancient days.
Forever seeing answers and yet so many questions.
We love and hug each other for another day.

OUR SPRING CONCERT

After 40 years I took up my tuba and joined Sitka Community Band. In my mind over those years I practiced fingerings remembering solos I did in high school music festivals. Now each concert I write something of early Sitka musical history for the program. Martin Strand

The rehearsals and performances of Fall and Winter are history.
Our musical building blocks have advanced the Band.
The multi-generational musicians work well together.
Tomorrow will be my 71st Spring in the love of music.
I am an enthusiastic believer in good Sitka Music.

My musical roots are deep in Sitka's history.
My mother, Lila and sister Sofia, were accomplished pianists.
They played the passionate "Poet and Peasant Overture."
The Sheldon Jackson Choir sang a life of beauty.
Southeast Music Festivals lift high our spirits.

The choirs of my youth sang "Ave Verum Corpus."
The Mozart masterpiece thrilled Sitka audiences.
It has a reverence and intensity we rarely hear today.
It is part of the Mozart "Requiem" July of 1791.
It is our pleasure to play an arrangement for band.
A cold April afternoon we played for the Fleet Blessing.
November 11 we play for the Veterans Banquet.
The 4th of July we are cheerfully part of the parade.
We look forward to our Christmas concert.
Being part of the musical community is our goal.

On the lawn of the Pioneer Home was my first concert.
My ancient dented tuba sprang to life after 40 years.
Being part of the band holds a special place in my life.
We experiment in musical harmony each Tuesday.
If you have loved music in your lifetime join us.

Martin R. Strand

SYMPHONY OF DEATH

Music has guided my life in times of trouble and stress.
There is a richness in its depth to reach my soul.
Today I will go to the library and take out the Fifth Symphony of
Shastakovich and listen to it in its entirety.

It speaks of the tragedy of death on a massive scale. It is a reflection
of my feelings about the World Trade Center disaster and the music
hammers on an exposed nerve as only Shostakovich can from his
personal experience.

My anger and rage continues measure after measure throughout the
symphony. However it offers some relief with a beautiful, sad flute
solo bringing hope for humanity. I walk through the sorrow of the
lost loved ones.

In New York as each day hope lessens, the heroic help that came and
died only adds to the grief and sorrows.

CHAPTER 6   SPORTS

THEY WERE LEGENDS IN
THEIR OWN TIME

We hailed their every success on the basketball court.
They carried us all the way with them.
We cheered with confidence each win or loss.
It was the journey in excitement we gladly took.

I first saw the Sitka ANB team play at the SJS gym at age 7.
World War II was moving on rapidly.
The windows of the gym were covered so no light came through.
Strong Native men with skill and finesse crafted a game.
They were all business winning for our Founders.

Peter Simpson was, in addition to his work, a coach.
At this time he was on the sidelines promoting their good work.
Helping in fund raising for Gold Medal Tournaments.
Florence Donnelly joined with cheerleaders for SJS.
It was a fast game with lots of clever moves.

Bounce the ball three times then pass to another girl.
Work your way down the court and give the ball
to Adeline Bartness under the key for two points.
She's fouled and got that last shot to win the game.
Such were the Sheldon Jackson Girl's team efforts in the early days.

Roland Wurster was the referee, not afraid to make a call.
He ruled with a missionary fairness with compassion.
Sportsmanship in those days was a high priority.
Double dribbles were a no-no and were caught every time.
Discipline was kept to the highest level.

Our elders were constant spectators at each thrilling game.
Often the scores were very close, often winning by one point.
The crowd would rise to its feet at a great play.
I would be at the half-way part of the bleachers cheering.
My brother, John Bashore and I would later walk home.

Basketball would be at the SJS gym, Etolin Street gym, and others.
I heard a basketball dribble while I was passing the SJS gym.
It was in the afternoon and Mo Johnson was all alone.
He was perfecting his long shots before three pointers.
It was pure poetry in motion just like ballet.

I have watched for decades before I became a photographer.
I brought back from Ohio State a Pentax H1 camera for sports.
Basketball games became a passion with me.
Photographing City League games and Tournaments
Was for quite a while a professional and personal interest.

In my early radio days I worked with Johnny Hope and Harry Lanz.
They were the broadcast team at all basketball games.
Later Howard Bradshaw did play-by-play here and in Juneau.
His broadcasts were colorful to say the least.
When Howard and Johnny teamed up that was something.

"This is Senator Howard Bradshaw along with Johnny Hope,
bringing you the game between Sitka ANB and the Juneau Arctic
Knights. The gym is filled with an overflow crowd of partisans from
both communities. I just came back from a break in Senate action
and I brought home some pork for Sitka and glad of it. How's the
game looking, Johnny?"

"Well, the score is tied at 68 to 68 with just two minutes to go. Juneau has possession of the ball and while we have a moment, lets take it back to Harry Lanz for a word from one of our sponsors."

"Thang you Thang you! Reeds Cash Market is bringing you this great game. Crosse and Blackwell canned Figgy pudding is only 77 cents until Friday. Turkey by the whole is 22 cents a pound. We're a small store with big ideas! Now back to the action, Johnny."

"This is Howard Bradshaw, Harry. Johnny went to get a can of pop. I think the Juneau ref was sent here only to protect his team. Mo gets fouled and was no where near the action. Here's Johnny"

"Juneau's coming down the floor and is intercepted by Merle Williams who passes it to Herby Didrickson who see's Mighty Mo Johnson in the clear 50 feet from the basket. Mo is set and Juneau sees his left foot drag as he lets fly one to win another Sitka ANB game. What a happy crowd!"

Decades of good basketball have enriched our lives in Sitka.
The cast of characters has changed over time
But the beauty of the game lives on in our memories.
We the willing crowd celebrate those precious memories.
Thankful we have a crowd tonight to share this celebration!

POOL AND RELOADING

Once I find myself thinking deeply about my past. Bitter sweet thoughts of what I could be if I tried. Everything tempered with the spice of reality. With a little more effort I could have increased my resources. Lingering in my thoughts of moving away from all this.

Putting distance from my problems could be good. But without the where-with-all is meaningless to me. My wealth would last perhaps 30 days at the most. I have so much baggage here to sort through. There is not enough time in my lifetime to sort.

If there was some spark of hope to get me going? The question comes up why and for what? Accepting the cards I was dealt seems the only way. In a life that is not really, a game is all I have. My path into the future looks so short.

In pool playing tonight I lost 7 straight games to Devin. My concentration was broken by sloppy pool on the other table. I have always said bad shooting is contagious and it was. I did win a few games by will power alone but not enough. Scratches on key balls was surely my downfall.

Let me analyze my technique at tonight's game. I shot too fast and did not take time to set up the shot. Shooting on instinct used to be my way but not any more. I have to make an effort to be excellent but tonight I failed. When I won I would count up to at least 4 before I made a shot. Counting to at least 10 is much better for planning a shot. It was painful being so stupid and careless. I have to have the will to win before I get to the pool hall.

It seems that I am pleased to get a difficult shot completed now and then. I challenge myself to do the hard shots sometimes at the expense of the easier ones. This is what I call playing "code of the

West." Most players do this by shooting in only one style and trying to make a ball every shot. One must realize that it is sometimes correct to miss a ball once in a while, looking to hide your opponent and buying yourself another shot. I thought about these things in advance of coming to the pool hall but forgot and paid for it by losing so many games in a row. I had to claw my way back to near the top for the rest of the evening.

My opponent, Devin, quietly and accurately continued the fame to his advantage. My inner rage at losing did harm to my game by the square root. But my defensive play should have kicked in much sooner. I did try some defensive moves but the cue ball drifted wrong and gave Devin an advantage. He is such a good sport throughout the evening and that helped calm my internal rage! I learned a painful and valuable lesson tonight.

You can always tell when I am concerned about my writing there are fewer paragraphs and thoughts run together trying to explain my sad fate.

Part of my creative life is on hold at present. My video editing software is not yet in town from Performance Entertainment (computer store). They gave me a used CD editing software but they had no serial number for it and I could not install lit. I paid $39.00 for it and it usually runs $49.00 new which they promised to get for me a month ago. I have my 30 gigabyte hard drive ready to put into my computer when the software is here. Then I will be doing video production. This will be a new direction in my life. I will have to start a catalog of background images to work with the serious work. NOTE, our video player has an annoying hum to it that might not stop. Perhaps, grounding under the house might work.

An edge off my wit occurred Saturday morning at 1504 Edgecumbe Drive. We were at that sale before 9 A. M. start time and Keith the gun dealer was already looking over the big box of reloading supplies. He would not let me look at it and put the things back and took the box to the sales lady. He asked me how much it might be worth and I told him to make an offer and I would counter offer.

He started at $60.00 and I raised to $65.00 he eventually got it at $75.00. There were several cans of gun powder (About 8 @ $18.00 retail). There were 380 brass and bullets (8 boxes of 100 @ $20.00). I should have kept the bidding going since I needed the powder especially. It could have been partial filled cans I don't know. But it was the best garage sale of reloading supplies this year.

POOL LEAGUE

Tuesday night the Pool League play is at the Columbia. We play team # 1 in the league, Columbia A. It is important that we use OUR TABLE! DO NOT LET THEM SUGGEST THAT WE USE THEIR TABLE! I can't stress this point enough. We should witness their drawing of names. We can select the rotation of our own team since Columbia Bar is our Home Table. I've talked to Dennis Bolin and he'll play for us.

ANOTHER BIRTHDAY PASSES

My 70th year is here and what will it bring?
My health is generally good and I am trying to stay in shape.
Just the other day I could have crashed my bike.
It was so sad that I had to ride with faulty equipment.
The brakes were not adjusted and did not work.

The corner of Lake and Sawmill was the scene.
As I came to the intersection at a good clip.
A bus was pulling away from the turn to Halibut point.
I hit the brakes all the way and nothing happened.
I was in the middle lane and pulled ahead of a car to the left.

It is a good thing that the car did not go forward.
I stopped at the "Thrift Shop" entrance and got off.
Such gross negligence of putting off the brake repair!
I wheeled the bike home from there dragging my tail.
I always wanted to be a safe driver but this time I failed.

The result of this problem is that I went home to fix the problem.
I took off both wheels and installed them on another frame.
I had to search for another brake pad to fit this bike.
I must have spent an hour on the project but it works.
And so goes another day in paradise!

On the upside I attended the 40-day party for Joe Peterson.
I did "Remembering the Spirit of Joe" for those present.
It was well received by the crowd and I was pleased.
It was the evening of March 26th to the morning of the 27th
I stayed for a few hours before dinner.

March 31st was the SEARHC memorial vigil.
I played my keyboard in the stairwell of the hospital.
"Vigil into the Night" my poem, I read to the opening service.
At John Brown's beach I read my work on early TB days.
It was good to meet my Southeast Tribal citizens.

Did I mention that our 8-Ball team Legion Native took 2nd place?
We had only 4 out of 5 of our team playing the #1 team in town.
I got 27 out of 30 balls and two magical games against our
opponents.
One was a complex 8 ball to the side pocket right on!
We, however, lost 133 to 77 which was good enough for 2nd place.

NINE BALL WISDOM

Some of the wisdom I know about 8 Ball and 9 Ball, I will give you an idea. I can see so many stereotypes played out on that table. Those with limited knowledge of the game tend to be filled with inflexible attitudes on what is right. They think the game must be approached in one way which I call "code of the West."

Bad shooting is definitely contagious, and is what I see all the time in town. Players tend to follow their opponent's bad habits. Namely, if their opponent shoots fast they shoot fast. I've noticed each shooter has a speed that is his very own. When they try to follow another player's performance they foul up their own. The best way to proceed is to try to find your own speed and accuracy.

A great percentage of shooters are not familiar with the rules. Almost every week I find someone is trying to use rules that are years old and have changed since then. It is possible to use the rules as a weapon! I also find that in any given team the team members have differing ideas on what rules to follow.

Those that use the rules correctly usually win. It seems to some such a hardship sitting down and discussing the finer points of the rules. Part of the problem is in writing the rules by our officers. There are a lot of fine points in the rules we were given. Also, we are given additional general rules which is a whole new ball game. It is necessary to those who care to learn both sets of rules.

I am disappointed with the Pool League officers having an only captains meeting. There are a lot of interested, skilled and learning players that could be helpful in having a say about the League. I think the top heavy team likes to keep control of League activities by limiting the general shooters away from learning about rules changes and they have the advantage. This is how it has been for decades of the League I'm sad to say.

There are lots of skillful players turned away because of the League rules. Some are lazy and don't want to learn the rules and would rather play code of the West. They say we just want to have fun! They never reach the higher level of competitive technique. I would like to have a skilled all star team travel to other pool tournaments around the country instead of having expensive trophies and a huge dinner. There is impending intimidation in several of the high score teams. Some of the lower teams think that they are unbeatable. Few of these general teams lack any defensive structure. There are many helpful techniques that can slow down a more skillful player from time to time. Hiding that cue ball and getting a ball--in--hand now and then can help.

Setting up your opponent to take a risky bank or full length table shot can be helpful. Just thinking of where you want the cue ball for the next shot can put you in better position. Use of the rake will increase your potential by at least 15 percent! Watching your game closely is valuable to catch errors of your opponent. Many players turn away and miss an error because they were not paying attention. Finally, there are very few times a player can practice by themselves to improve a wide variety of techniques. Please try to take time for your own practice!

NINE BALL GAME

Sometimes my best efforts are not enough. This competitive game goes on sometimes without me. December 10, 2004

I walked too far into the night last night.
I had hoped I could perform perfectly at 9 ball but fell far short.
The pool table was well worn at the American Legion.
The cue ball would endlessly bounce off the rails into the unknown.
We had little control after taking a shot.

I desperately tried to hide the ball from my opponents but each shot failed.
It would roll and roll for a perfect set up for the other guy.
In order to perfect my performance, I would have to practice very often.
The table needs to be re-surfaced with fresh felt upgrade.
Some of the rails are loose and making banking a shot difficult.

I am seriously considering quitting the 9 ball league play.
Maybe I stayed too long at the Fair?
The demands of my skill are very much taxed to the limit.
I was, unfortunately, just one of the boys last night.
My competitive spirit shot out the window in defeat.

Here I am complaining about the equipment!
It is a poor workman that blames his tools!
I do not have the resources to practice the necessary work.
This is an indicator of my failing skill level.
Is age a factor in this growing malaise?

Using all the tricks I could think of in the game, I failed.
My stop shots rolled further than I expected.
My attempts to hide the ball never happened.
The straight in shots veered off to parts unknown.
The bank shots were all less than perfect.

My opponents played a no nonsense game throughout.

A FRESH, NEW OUTLOOK

Flashing deep into my memory your face is revealed.
Twelve, lonely years disappear at your touch.
Your intense and sincere expression reflected your love.
Filling my life with hope I stammer some words.
When our hug ended you gave me a new energy.

You were so young then and now you are woman.
Your beauty comes from your inside and out.
Deeper than only friendship we looked good together.
My sadness is that my sunshine years are dimming.
What lies ahead for us?

I cheer your life and your expectations.
My star is already light years out in space.
Your star is bright and will shine a long time.
There are other stars near you that sparkle.
Fewer stars are at the edge of my universe.

To remember how good we were is enough.
The talks and my blossoms of piano music evolved.
The creative time of my life was beginning.
You did all the right things for your growing life.
My smile deepens as I am filled with remembering.

My resources are few to carry me to the future.
My life nearly spent, but spent well.
How much better it might have been?
Now I am content just to make TODAY work.
A man that lived well and enjoyed your specialness.

I now sit and compose beautiful words and occasionally music.
Inspiration comes easily when I think of you.
In musical meditation I frame your lovely life.
A rustling in my universe blinks with strong feeling.
She is here!

CONCLUSION

As you have read carefully through all the articles that Martin wrote you might have noticed the theme, sometimes so subtly hidden, of a desire to really make a difference. He raises the question about the ultimate value to his life, and of his life to his many and varied occupations or interests. He saw in his grandfather, Ralph Young not only a deep cultural awareness but also a religious purpose where God and his relation to God is ultimately of importance. Martin saw this in his grandparents and likewise sees it in himself. Faith makes a difference.

As Martin has reached back through his generations to find meaning there is the almost quiet desire to have made a difference. It is as though he has been walking through the darkness with many lights shining and just to the side he sees his shadow, occasionally on one side and then on the other, sometimes walking behind him, sometimes with him and often in front of him, but always tied to himself through his feet.

His ability to see into and through a personality to the depth of meaning, the central purpose for life for each individual and for himself was one of the outstanding things about Martin. It is this editor's hope that the reader will be able to sit back and "muse" your own way through your life so far. As Martin sought an ultimate purpose, to what purpose has the reader put his or her life? You can even sit back in the midst of beautiful music, as did Martin and let the music guide you.

Martin's purpose in life will have been achieved if the reader assimilates or develops Martin's sense of concern for other individuals, regardless of their culture, status or position, and sees them as unique persons.